Nobody's Perfect,
but You Have to Be

NOBODY'S PERFECT, BUT *You* HAVE TO BE

The Power of Personal Integrity in Effective Preaching

DEAN SHRIVER

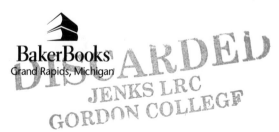

BakerBooks
Grand Rapids, Michigan

Published by Baker Books
a division of Baker Publishing Group
P.O. Box 6287, Grand Rapids, MI 49516-6287
www.bakerbooks.com

Printed in the United States of America

Library of Congress Cataloging-in-Publication Data
Shriver, Dean, 1954–
    Nobody's perfect, but you have to be : the power of personal integrity in effective preaching / Dean Shriver.
            p.   cm.
    Includes bibliographical references.
    ISBN 0-8010-9182-9 (pbk.)
    1. Preaching. 2. Integrity—Religious aspects—Christianity. 3. Clergy—Conduct of life. I. Title.
BV4211.3.S55 2005
253'.2—dc22   2004021439

To Nancy—you are a woman of integrity
and God's gift to me.

Contents

Part 3: How Integrity Grows

FOREWORD

There's a cynical remark making the rounds these days. "Integrity is everything! Once you have learned to fake that everything else is easy." In our culture genuine integrity seems as scarce as polar bears in the Sahara.

Integrity is hard to find in politics. Spinning the facts, or actually lying about them, has become standard operational procedure. No one expects campaign promises to be kept after the candidate gets into office. Ugly rumors designed to destroy an opponent or his family are the poisoned fruit of politics.

The warning, "Let the buyer beware," tells us that integrity isn't a big commodity in the marketplace either. For instance, hucksters, like old-fashioned medicine men, tout the health benefits of their products on the front of the box, but the back of the box in much smaller print tells us that the claim is actually a fraud. For years the tobacco industry insisted, "There is no supporting evidence that smoking is harmful to your health." Yet when it was proved that they lied, and they had known for years that cigarettes caused cancer and other life-destroying diseases, they didn't close down their operations as integrity would demand. Instead, they shifted their market to people in Europe, Africa, and Asia. When your only principle is protect the bottom line, then integrity goes up in smoke.

A significant percentage of Americans do not trust the integrity of the media. Newspaper reporters have confessed to inventing their stories, making up quotes or manufacturing interviews to enhance their careers. Newspaper editorials so often present opinion as fact that readers come to read facts as merely opinion.

In a culture where integrity seems like a fool's game, only the naive seal a deal with a promise and a handshake. Instead the shrewd call in a lawyer to write up a contract. But a contract isn't necessarily binding. Professional athletes sign their contracts, but don't have the integrity to keep them. They want to "renegotiate" whenever they feel it is to their advantage. Wise readers learn to take out a magnifying glass to read the small print in contracts or brochures. Airlines and travel agencies lure travelers with the giant letters and the four-color pictures on the top of the page, but take away what they appear to give in the tiny print at the bottom of the page.

You don't have to be a cynic to doubt the claims made to us every day in a sincere voice and with a straight face.

> "I'm calling for the telephone company to tell you about a new calling plan designed only to save you money."
>
> "The merger of these two great banks will cut costs, expand productivity, and provide our customers with better service without laying off one single person."
>
> "The new tax cut will benefit every man, woman, and child in America."
>
> "If I am your leader, I will create ten million good paying jobs."
>
> "You can be sure that this university has never offered a star high school player anything more than room and board to recruit him."
>
> "Use our exercise machine just ten minutes a day and you will lose twenty pounds in a month without dieting."
>
> "As the lawyer of the accused all I am asking for is justice."

"Try this diet supplement for thirty days and if you are not
completely satisfied, return it to us and we will cheerfully
refund your money."

When we are constantly lied to, is there anyplace we can find
integrity?

How about the church? On Sunday mornings pastors preach
about integrity. But regrettably the clerical collar has become not
only a symbol of honor but also of child abuse. "Television evan-
gelist" is synonym for hypocrite and fraud. Many local congregations have been torn apart by shepherds who lacked integrity. They
have betrayed the people in their care. These leaders have ignored
God's warning, "Woe to the shepherds of Israel who only take care
of themselves! Should not the shepherds take care of the flock?"
(Ezek. 34:2).

How then can we be heard in these wilderness times crying for
a voice? Dean Shriver reminds us again of the need for personal
integrity in preachers and their preaching. He argues that integrity
is everything, and it must not be faked. While we can't be perfect, we
must be genuine to be believed. The God who speaks with utmost
integrity must have messengers who represent him well. Anyone in
ministry, therefore, needs to read this book. Although it can be read
in a couple of hours, it will have to be practiced for a lifetime.

Haddon W. Robinson
Harold John Ockenga Distinguished Professor of Preaching
Gordon-Conwell Theological Seminary

ACKNOWLEDGMENTS

This book is a product of grace—God's grace expressed through those who love, support, and encourage me. First among them is my wife, Nancy. At times she has, without complaint, played the role of single mom to make this project possible. Her love is patient. My children—Michael, Rebekah, and Kristen—shared in this sacrifice with her. They are God's blessing to me. I love them deeply.

I am grateful to my parents, Philip K. and Madeline Shriver, both for modeling a life of integrity before me and for letting me hang out with them while working on my initial draft. For two months they opened their hearts and their guesthouse to me. Accommodations included laundry service and meals. It was just like old times!

I can never adequately express my gratitude to my spiritual family at Intermountain Baptist Church. First, they provided me with a two-month writing sabbatical. More important, for the past eighteen years they have patiently loved me as we have all struggled together to grow up in Christ. No pastor has been more blessed in ministry than I have.

Both Haddon Robinson and Sid Buzzell reviewed my initial manuscript and offered suggestions that shaped the final form of this book. To his review of the manuscript, Haddon Robinson added his encouragement and support.

I am grateful to God for the way he ministers to me through so many.

INTRODUCTION

You must have holiness; and dear brethren, if you should fail in
mental qualifications (as I hope you will not), and if you should
have a slender measure of the oratorical faculty (as I trust you will
not), yet depend on it, a holy life is in itself a wonderful power,
and will make up for many deficiencies; it is in fact the best sermon
the best man can deliver.

C. H. Spurgeon, *Lectures to My Students* [1]

The worship service was about to begin when I saw her. I greeted
her with curiosity. I knew she was a fully committed member of
a sister church in our area. During our brief exchange she quietly
said, "I simply cannot listen to that man preach." That man was her
pastor of almost two years. Why, on that morning, did she refuse
to hear her own pastor preach? Was he a heretical teacher? Did he
deny the truth of God's Word? Did he habitually twist Scripture
to suit his own desires? No, on that Sunday the woman I greeted
refused to hear her pastor because of his actions, not his words. It
had happened at a recent board meeting. In the midst of debating
an issue the young pastor exploded in anger, slandered the woman's
husband (a well-respected elder thirty years his senior), and even
threatened to excommunicate him from the church. In the days
that followed, the pastor continued to malign her husband behind

15

his back. Now, at least in this woman's eyes, the young minister's credibility as a preacher was destroyed. On that Sunday morning, it wasn't that she could not hear him—she would not.

Each Sunday our congregations hear the sermon we preach. The rest of the week they see the sermon we live. If these two sermons don't coincide, it's doubtful the people we minister to will really listen when we preach. More doubtful still is that God will use our preaching to radically transform their lives. The preaching God uses to change lives requires more than accurate exegesis, clear purpose statements, creative sermon design, and impressive delivery. As pastors, our actions outside the pulpit are as critical to effective preaching as the words we proclaim while in the pulpit.

More than three hundred years before Christ, Aristotle wrote, "It is not true, as some writers assume in their treatises on rhetoric, that the personal goodness revealed by the speaker contributes nothing to his power of persuasion; on the contrary, his character may almost be called the most effective means of persuasion he possesses."[2] The principle Aristotle recognized is a biblical principle basic to preaching. When all is said and done, credible preaching requires credible preachers. And credible preachers are those who possess integrity. The root meaning of the word *integrity* is "intact." Integrity is "the state of being whole or undivided."[3] Specifically, we as preachers demonstrate integrity when unity exists between the truth we proclaim and the lives we live. Simply put, integrity exists when we consistently "practice what we preach."

Integrity is crucial to our preaching. Integrity is more crucial than a well-crafted introduction. It's more crucial than smooth delivery. In preaching, integrity is always more crucial than technique because all the oratory skill on earth can never transfuse spiritual power into a sermon bled dry by a preacher's own contradictory life.

In America today the church of Jesus Christ is struggling. It is common for our teenagers to engage in premarital sex. Evangelical adults divorce and remarry regularly in spite of the fact that Jesus calls the practice "adultery" (Matt. 5:32; 19:1–12). And even though most professing believers verbally acknowledge that this world is not their home, their lives are still consumed by the pursuit of comfort and ever-higher standards of living.

In light of this, we preachers need to ask ourselves some tough questions. Could it be that the substandard conduct marking the lives of many professing Christians is due—at least in part—to the conduct they see modeled by their pastors? Is it possible that the light of the church has grown dim in the world because the light of preachers has grown dim in the church? We proclaim the authority of God's Word. Do we personally submit to that authority in full view of our congregations? We preach Christ's life-changing power. Do our hearers see that power visibly working in our lives? In other words, do our congregations see unity between the truth we preach and the lives we live? Do they see integrity?

This book is for preaching pastors and for those pursuing that call. I write because of my own need to continually return home to one elementary truth—the life I live as a preacher can never be isolated from the truth I proclaim. For better or worse, the congregation I serve does more than hear me. They watch me. And the impact of what they hear will, to a large degree, be determined by what they see in my life.

As you read this book, I pray that you will join me in remembering both the privilege of hearing God's call to preach and the responsibility we have to answer his call fully. The first section of the book (chapters 1–3) reminds us that the call to preach is a call to integrity. Integrity is critical to our present task of preaching, to our own eternal well-being, and to the eternal well-being of our hearers. The second section of the book (chapters 4–11) offers a practical definition of biblical integrity followed by an examination of seven character traits that mark a life of integrity. The third section (chapters 12–14) encourages the pursuit of integrity by means of spiritual disciplines, expository preaching, and longevity in God's chosen place of ministry.

Nobody's perfect—and no, we really don't have to be. But, as preachers, we must be genuine. We must possess integrity because, in preaching, enduring effectiveness always demands consistency between the life we live and the truth we proclaim.

PART 1

WHY INTEGRITY COUNTS

1

INTEGRITY'S POWER TO PERSUADE

Your temper is uneven; you lack love for your neighbors. You grow angry too easily; your tongue is too sharp—thus the people will not hear you.

John Wesley to a Methodist minister, *The Works of John Wesley*[1]

In Utah they're known as the "Plaza Preachers." They regularly take their place directly in front of the Salt Lake Mormon Temple on the Main Street Plaza. They shout through megaphones, sometimes calling Mormon passersby harlots and whores. When Mormon wedding parties ask them to move further down the plaza so bridal pictures can be taken, they refuse. When queried by reporters, they explain that their obnoxious behavior is part of their "Christian duty." With their words, they offer Christ's love. By their actions, they close the hearts of their hearers to that love. Instead of drawing Latter-day Saints to Jesus, they most often drive them away. Because no integrity exists between their message and their conduct, these plaza preachers have forever convinced their listeners that they have nothing credible to say.

This is the tragedy of all who preach with their lips but not with their lives. Preaching God's Word is by nature a form of persuasive speech. It is a well-established principle of communication that persuasive speech is seldom effective if the speaker is not deemed credible. Credibility requires integrity.

During the first century, Roman rhetorician Quintilian wrote, "I not only say that he who would answer my idea of an orator must be a good man, but that no man, unless he be good, can ever be an orator."[2] Explaining further he adds, "for bad men, as well in their pleadings as in their lives, entertain dishonest expectations; and it often happens, *that even when they speak the truth, belief is not accorded them*, and the employment of advocates of such character is regarded as a proof of the badness of a cause" (emphasis mine).[3]

The tactics employed by Utah's plaza preachers demonstrate their lack of integrity. Their lack of integrity is now regarded by Mormons as "proof of the badness" of their cause. The tragic result is, as Quintilian says, "that even when they speak the truth, belief is not accorded them."

But even as a lack of integrity serves to turn people from truth, the opposite is also true. Integrity's presence in the life of a preacher can powerfully draw people to the truth. Integrity persuades! The power of consistency between a message and the life of the one who proclaims it was clearly demonstrated over the course of eighteen hours one fall day in 1943. America was at war. For a third time, radio star Kate Smith volunteered to serve as spokesperson in a government war bond drive. Describing the bond drive, communication researcher Robert Merton wrote:

> September 21, 1943 was War Bond Day for Columbia Broadcasting System. During a span of eighteen hours—from eight o'clock that morning until two the next morning—a radio star named Kate Smith spoke for a minute or two at repeated intervals . . . On sixty-five distinct occasions in the course of the day, she begged, cajoled, demanded that her listeners buy war bonds. Within the narrow borders of her brief messages, Smith managed to touch upon a variety of themes enshrined in American culture . . . Apparently, there was nothing here of a cut and dried radio script.

This was presented as a personal message, iterated and reiterated in a voice often broken, it seemed, by deep emotion. And people did more than listen.[4]

How much more they did is nothing short of incredible. During her first war bond drive Smith raised $1 million in pledges. In her second drive she netted $2 million. Unbelievably, during the eighteen hours of her third drive she sold war bonds totaling $39 million! What made Kate Smith so much more persuasive during her third bond drive than her previous two? By surveying listeners who heard Smith, Merton discovered that the entertainer's credibility as a spokesperson was the key that moved so many to act on her appeal. But what was the key to her credibility? It was the public's perception that she willingly sacrificed for the good of American soldiers even as she called on them to sacrifice. Smith's willingness to work without pay and to endure the full eighteen hours of the drive without sleep convinced the public of her integrity. Merton comments on Smith's willingness to work without pay:

> Within this context appears the conviction of her listeners that she was not paid for her all-day broadcasts during the war bond drive, as indeed she was not. The readiness, in our commercial civilization, to serve without pay was taken as the very touchstone of sincerity and disinterestedness.[5]

Regarding Smith's long workday, Merton continues:

> Above all, the presumed stress and strain of the eighteen-hour series of broadcasts served to validate Smith's sincerity. *The deed, not the word, furnished the ostensible proof.* Not merely the content of her messages, but the fact of the all-day drive, believed to be unique in radio history, was taken to testify to her distinctive willingness to serve (emphasis mine).[6]

Merton later observes:

> Viewed as a process of persuasion, the marathon converted initial feelings of skepticism and doubt among listeners into a reluctant,

and then, a full-fledged acceptance of Smith's integrity. The successive broadcasts served as a fulfillment in action of a promise in words.[7]

As each hour passed, Smith's credibility—and her persuasive power—grew. One listener described her own change in attitude:

At eight in the morning, she said, "This is Kate Smith and I'm going to talk to you every fifteen minutes as long as my voice holds out." I thought, "Hmph, she hasn't begun talking yet and she's talking about quitting already." *I've been getting fed up with all the big names getting all the credit for war work.* I thought she regarded it as a job she had to do. *Later she seemed really sincere. My reaction changed favorably, not because of what she was saying, but because she was still at it.* After about the eighth appeal I began to listen more whole-heartedly. Then I got furious at myself that a little thing like her interrupting one of my favorite programs should have annoyed me. I laughed at myself too. I thought, "You don't like Kate Smith, and here you are staying in to hear her." *After listening to her for so long I thought she had integrity. She kept her promise.*[8]

Merton concludes:

The marathon, then, reinforced the appropriateness of Smith as a salesman of war bonds. *By this act, she earned the right to speak.* She was not subjected to resentment leveled at others who lack the moral authority to make demands in the name of the nation (emphasis mine).[9]

What can we learn from Kate Smith's war bond drive? Certainly, no preacher can establish enduring credibility in a church in a matter of eighteen hours. Still, the lesson is clear. By her deeds Kate Smith gained "the moral authority to make demands in the name of the nation." Have we, by our deeds, gained the moral authority required to speak credibly in God's name? When we call on our congregation to sacrifice for Christ's cause, they silently ask if we have sacrificed first. Have we? When we call them to be holy like God is holy, they look for holiness in our lives too. Will they find it there?

When we preach that pride must give way to humility, they ask if that's really possible. Then they look for the answer in our example.

It's no wonder that when Paul writes Timothy he exhorts the young preacher to "set an example for the believers in life, in love, in faith, and in purity," and to "watch your life and doctrine closely" (1 Tim. 4:12, 16).

By God's design, the Word preached has little transforming power apart from the life and example of the preacher. Persuasion requires credibility and credibility requires integrity. Integrity is the consistency that exists between our message and our lives when we do, in fact, watch *both* our lives and our doctrine closely. Phillips Brooks reminds us:

> Whatever strange and scandalous eccentricities the ministry has sometimes witnessed, this is certainly true, and is always encouraging, that no man permanently succeeds in it who cannot make men believe that he is pure and devoted, *and the only sure and lasting way to make men believe in one's devotion and purity is to be what one wishes to be believed to be* (emphasis mine).[10]

God's Word persuades most powerfully not only when it is heard, but when it is both heard and seen in the life of the one who proclaims it.

2

REVISITING GOD'S CALL

The preacher must be a godly man . . . It is only after emphasizing such qualities that we come to the question of ability. It seems to me to be one of the tragedies of the modern Church that we tend to put ability first.

D. Martyn Lloyd-Jones, *Preaching and Preachers*[1]

I tossed and turned, fighting to ignore the voice in my head. We had plans. In six months I would leave the air force but remain in this city we loved. I would teach school and perhaps fly with the Washington Air Guard. Nancy and I would raise our family in Spokane. It promised to be a good and comfortable life. But in the darkness I could not dam up the river of words that cascaded through my mind. They were Christ's words. "If anyone would come after me, he must deny himself and take up his cross and follow me." I plugged my heart's ears, but the volume only increased. "Whoever wants to save his life will lose it, but whoever loses his life for me will find it. What good will it be for a man if he gains the whole world yet forfeits his soul?" I steadied my breathing and again sought sleep, but the stream continued to flow. "If anyone

27

comes to me and does not hate his father and mother, his wife and children, his brothers and sisters—yes, even his own life—he cannot be my disciple." Another hour dragged by, but his words raced on—"Any of you who does not give up everything he has cannot be my disciple." Then, for just one moment, there was silence. The ultimatum was not audible, but it was real. Out of the silence he spoke in my heart—"Do what I say or stop calling yourself a Christian." It was over. For seven years I had run. For seven years he had relentlessly (and mercifully) pursued me. Hopelessly cornered on a sleepless May night in 1982, I answered God's call to preach.

The call to preach breaks into a life in many different ways. For some, God's call involves a dramatic event that immediately changes the course of one's future. For others it begins with a whisper and slowly grows into the settled conviction that a life invested in proclaiming the truth is the only life that will satisfy. Still others acknowledge God's call to preach only after fellow believers encourage them to recognize the presence of spiritual gifts they may not have initially been aware of.

Whatever means God uses, *how* he calls someone to preach is not nearly so critical as understanding *what* his call entails. The call to preach is rightly viewed as a call to do something. It is the "doing" the apostle Paul had in mind when the approaching storm of martyrdom compelled him to exhort Timothy, his protégé, to "discharge all the duties of your ministry" (2 Tim. 4:5b). Chief among these duties of ministry is, "Preach the Word; be prepared in season and out of season; correct, rebuke and encourage—with great patience and careful instruction" (2 Tim. 4:2).

God's call to preach, then, is a call to do something critically important. The problem is that's where we often stop. Scripture is clear. In the ministry of preaching, *doing*, by itself, is not enough. Answering God's call to preach is also about *being*! To know this we need look no further than the ministry of Christ himself. Jesus is our model for ministry. Jesus is God's perfect preacher. We can never know what it means to fully answer God's call to preach until we see how Jesus answered it. Introducing Jesus as "the Word," John's Gospel informs us:

In the beginning was the Word, and the Word was with God, and the Word was God . . . The Word became flesh and made his dwelling among us. We have seen his glory, the glory of the One and Only, who came from the Father, full of grace and truth . . . No one has ever seen God, but God the One and Only, who is at the Father's side, has made him known.

John 1:1, 14, 18

Jesus Christ, the Word, made his dwelling among us. He came full of grace and truth. He communicated. He preached. He made the Father known. How? John chapter 1 tells us. Jesus, the perfect preacher, communicated God's life-changing Word not just by speaking the truth but also by *being* the truth in our midst. Yes, the words of Jesus preached. But so did his life! In Christ's earthly ministry the Word wasn't just heard, it was seen. The apostle John's account of Jesus' sermon on servanthood demonstrates this.

It was just before the Passover Feast. Jesus knew that the time had come for him to leave this world and go to the Father. Having loved his own who were in the world, he now showed them the full extent of his love. The evening meal was served, and the devil had already prompted Judas Iscariot, son of Simon, to betray Jesus. Jesus knew that the Father had put all things under his power, and that he had come from God and was returning to God; so he got up from the meal, took off his outer clothing, and wrapped a towel around his waist. After that, he poured water into a basin and began to wash his disciples' feet, drying them with the towel that was wrapped around him.

John 13:1–5

In this account we must remember, Jesus isn't simply playing the role of a servant for the sake of making a point. Jesus *is* a servant by nature. Jesus isn't *using* an object lesson to teach. Jesus *is* the object lesson. In John 13, not only is Jesus calling his disciples to do what he does, he is calling them to be what he is at heart—a servant. Having demonstrated God's call to servanthood by his example, Jesus now verbalizes that call in verses 12–17:

When he had finished washing their feet, he put on his clothes and returned to his place. "Do you understand what I have done for you?" he asked them. "You call me 'Teacher' and 'Lord,' and rightly so, for that is what I am. Now that I, your Lord and Teacher, have washed your feet, you also should wash one another's feet. *I have set you an example that you should do as I have done for you.* I tell you the truth, no servant is greater than his master, nor is a messenger greater than the one who sent him. Now that you know these things, you will be blessed if you do them."

When Jesus preached to his disciples about the serving nature of Christian love, he not only spoke the message so they could hear it—he was the message so they could see it. This was the pattern of Jesus' entire preaching ministry. Jesus declared, "Greater love has no one than this, that he lay down his life for his friends,"[2] and then he laid down his own life for them. He promised, "I am the resurrection and the life,"[3] and then he conquered death. He commanded his disciples, "Go and make disciples of all nations,"[4] but only after they saw him reach out to the Samaritans and to a Canaanite woman.[5] He preached love for one's enemies, and he washed the feet of Judas. He instructed the repentant to "stop sinning,"[6] and he never sinned at all. Nowhere is the call to preach more clearly defined as a call to both speak and *be* God's message than in the life and ministry of Jesus himself. Jonathan Edwards reminds us:

> God sent His Son into the world to be the light of the world in two ways—by revealing his mind and will to the world, and also by setting the world a perfect example. So ministers are set to be lights, not only as teachers but as examples to the flock. The same things that ministers recommend to their hearers in doctrine, they should also show them an example in their practice.[7]

Of course, it would be lunacy to suggest that anyone called to preach can *be* God's message to the perfect extent Jesus was. Still, in Christ's example, God reveals his design for the perfect sermon. That design is incarnational. Even as pastors are called to speak God's message to a congregation, they are called to be God's message in the midst of that congregation. If our lives do not proclaim the truth as loudly as our lips, we have not fully answered God's call to preach.

Adopting Jesus' model, Paul understood that his preaching ministry encompassed both his verbal proclamation and his conduct. First Thessalonians 1–2 makes this clear. In 1 Thessalonians 1:4–5, Paul asserts that his righteous conduct was a critical element that empowered his preaching. He writes, "For we know, brothers loved by God that he has chosen you, because our gospel came to you not simply with words, but also with power, with the Holy Spirit and with deep conviction. *You know how we lived among you for your sake.*"

"You know how we lived among you for your sake." At first brush, the attention Paul draws to his own conduct, and that of his companions, seems out of place in a passage that speaks of the Holy Spirit's power to enlighten and convict whenever God's Word is preached. If this seems so, it is because we often envision the workings of God's Spirit to be mysterious and invisible. In the salvation of sinners the Spirit's work is in fact mysterious, but seldom is it invisible. This is because God has chosen to use his children as channels through which the Spirit's transforming power flows. When the Holy Spirit blesses an unbeliever with life-changing conviction of sin and the reality of grace through faith in Christ, he rarely, if ever, does so apart from a human messenger. This is always the case in the ministry of preaching.

That's why Paul points to his own life and conduct when reflecting on the Thessalonians' conversion. It was the integrity of Paul and his companions the Holy Spirit used to demonstrate the gospel's power even as that power was proclaimed. It was the apostle's righteousness the Spirit used to convict his hearers of sin. This is why Paul refused to separate "the life he lived among them" from his preaching of the gospel "with power, with the Holy Spirit and with deep conviction." The word Paul preached could not be isolated from the life he lived.

In 1 Thessalonians 2:3–13, Paul reiterates this truth:

> For the appeal we make does not spring from error or impure motives, nor are we trying to trick you. On the contrary, we speak as

men approved by God to be entrusted with the gospel. We are not trying to please men but God, who tests our hearts. You know we never used flattery, nor did we put on a mask to cover up greed—God is our witness. We were not looking for praise from men, not from you or anyone else.

As apostles of Christ we could have been a burden to you, but we were gentle among you, like a mother caring for her little children. We loved you so much that we were delighted to share with you not only the gospel of God but our lives as well, because you had become so dear to us. Surely you remember, brothers, our toil and hardship; we worked night and day in order not to be a burden to anyone while we preached the gospel of God to you.

You are our witnesses, and so is God, of how holy, righteous and blameless we were among you who believed. For you know that we dealt with each of you as a father deals with his own children, encouraging, comforting and urging you to live lives worthy of God, who calls you into his kingdom and glory.

And we also thank God continually because, when you received the word of God, which you heard from us, you accepted it not as the word of men, but as it actually is, the word of God, which is at work in you who believe.

Why can't we separate our personal character from the message we proclaim? Because our character gives evidence that our message is true. That's Paul's point. He reminds the Thessalonians that he and his companions refused to make their appeal out of "error or impure motives." They did not use flattery or "a mask to cover up greed." Rather, they were gentle with their hearers "like a mother caring for her little children" and dealt with them "as a father deals with his own children."

God used Paul's preaching to change eternal destinies because Paul committed himself to a life of integrity that both validated and empowered his preaching. This commitment to personal integrity marked Paul's entire ministry. In 2 Timothy 3:14 he speaks of himself, as well as Timothy's mother and grandmother, when he writes, "But as for you, continue in what you have learned and have become convinced of, *because you know those from whom you learned it.*" In his Corinthian ministry, Paul lived carefully so as to put "no stumbling block in anyone's path, so that our ministry might not be discredited."[8]

Perhaps the most surprising, and challenging, expression of Paul's commitment to preach with integrity was his practice of purposely calling attention to his own conduct. Twice he pleads with the Corinthians, "Imitate me!"[9] To the Philippians he writes, "Join with others in following my example."[10] In the same epistle he continues, "Whatever you have learned or received or heard from me, *or seen in me*—put into practice."[11] I fear, coming from many of us, such pleas might sound arrogant or, even worse, ridiculous. As preachers we must ask ourselves, "Can I confidently say to my hearers, 'Imitate me'?" And what if they did? Would God be pleased?

But wait! Paul was an apostle. Can we legitimately say that God demands the same standard of conduct from us that he expected of a specially chosen servant like Paul? Apparently so. The author of Hebrews assumes that all preachers, like Paul, will model the truth they proclaim when he writes, "Remember your leaders, who spoke the word of God to you. Consider the outcome of their way of life *and imitate their faith*."[12]

In light of this expectation that preachers will both speak God's message to their congregations and be God's message in the midst of those congregations, it is no surprise that the biblical qualifications for eldership (including preaching elders) emphasize character more than skill. According to 1 Timothy 3:1–6, an elder must be: above reproach, the husband of one wife, temperate, self-controlled, respectable, hospitable, able to teach, not given to drunkenness, not violent but gentle, not quarrelsome, not a lover of money, must manage his own family well, must not be a recent convert, and must have a good reputation with outsiders. As one commentator states, "In each case the focal point is the candidate's reputation among believers and unbelievers, which is to be computed on the basis of proven moral character and maturity. Duties are hardly mentioned."[13]

In light of this, Paul's words to Timothy in 1 Timothy 4:11–16 come as no surprise. It is in this passage that Paul most clearly defines the call to preach as a call to *both* speak and "be" God's word.

In the context of battling false teachers, Paul instructs Timothy to "command and teach" God's truth (v. 11). But Timothy is a relatively young man. Some in the church may question his right as pastor to "command and teach" them anything. By what means is Timothy instructed to gain the hearing he needs? What will make his preaching effective? The apostle answers, "Don't let anyone look down on you because you are young, *but set an example* for the believers in speech, in life, in love, in faith, and in purity. Until I come, devote yourself to the public reading of Scripture, to preaching and teaching."

In the battle against false teaching, Paul charges Timothy not only to preach truth with his lips, but also with his life. Timothy's authority and effectiveness as a preacher would not be established merely by proclaiming God's Word. He must model its application. Rather than demand a hearing, the young pastor was instructed to win a hearing by means of his example—his *typos*. Thayer defines the technical meaning of this Greek word as "the pattern in conformity to which a thing must be made."[14] The implication is clear. A preacher is called to do more than simply proclaim truth. He is called to live a model Christian life. His pattern of conduct must be worthy of imitation by believers younger in the faith than he. His life must be a visual demonstration of what living for Christ means.

Answering God's call to preach, then, necessarily requires the marriage of God's proclaimed Word to the life and conduct of the one proclaiming it. In 1 Timothy 4:15–16, Paul concludes his charge to the young pastor, instructing, "Be diligent in these matters; give yourself wholly to them, so that everyone may see your progress. Watch your *life and doctrine* closely. Persevere in them, because if you do, you will save both yourself and your hearers."

But it is not only in the positive examples of preachers like Paul and Timothy that we discover how important holy conduct is to preaching. The importance of a preacher's integrity is also demonstrated in the negative example of false teachers. It is significant that the New Testament often defines false teachers more by their deeds than their doctrine. With his aim trained squarely on false teachers, the apostle Peter writes:

They will be paid back with harm for the harm they have done.
Their idea of pleasure is to carouse in broad daylight. They are
blots and blemishes, reveling in their pleasures while they feast
with you. With eyes full of adultery, they never stop sinning; they
seduce the unstable; they are experts in greed—an accursed brood!
. . . They promise them freedom, while they themselves are slaves of
depravity—for a man is a slave to whatever has mastered him. [15]

Likewise, Jude 4 describes false teachers as "godless men, who
change the grace of God into a license for immorality." Here we
learn that God's people can most often judge the integrity of a
message by the integrity of the one who proclaims it. Nonetheless, a word of caution is in order. Because God's Word possesses a
power of its own, its life-changing potential is never bound to the
character of the preacher in an absolute sense. The Bible does offer
examples of truth being effectively proclaimed by evil men. Even
though Balaam is described by Peter as one "who loved the wages
of wickedness," [16] he still proclaimed a series of divinely inspired
oracles God used to bless Israel and curse the nations surrounding
them. [17] Likewise, Caiaphas, a wicked man who plotted the death
of Christ, prophesied under the direction of the Holy Spirit. [18] In
Philippians 1:12–18, Paul rejoices that the good news is preached
even when the preachers are motivated by envy, rivalry, selfish
ambition, and insincerity. Paul's joy over such preaching seems
anchored in his knowledge that God's Word does, in fact, possess
an innate power of its own. This is the power Isaiah 55:10–11 speaks
of when God promises:

> As the rain and the snow come down from heaven, and do not
> return to it without watering the earth and making it bud and
> flourish . . . so is my word that goes out from my mouth: It will not
> return to me empty, but will accomplish what I desire and achieve
> the purpose for which I sent it.

Likewise, in Jeremiah 23:29, God proclaims, "Is not my word
like fire . . . and like a hammer that breaks a rock in pieces?" In the

New Testament, Hebrews 4:12 describes the Word of God as being "living and active—sharper than any double-edged sword."

By God's sovereign power, his Word can penetrate hearts and change lives even when it is proclaimed by godless men. Still, a careful study of Scripture leaves little doubt that a life-changing proclamation of God's Word *in spite of* a preacher's character is not God's normal way of working. In the context of Isaiah 55:10–11, God's Word, which "does not return void," is preached by a prophet specifically called and purified for his task (see Isa. 6:1–8). In Jeremiah 23:29, where God's Word is declared to be "like fire" and "a hammer that breaks a rock in pieces," the Lord is rebuking false prophets who will not preach that powerful Word *because* of their character flaws. And in the case of those wrongly motivated evangelists mentioned by Paul, it is likely that theirs was an itinerant ministry in which their character was not known well enough to either add to or detract from their proclamation of truth. As pastors committed to living among and preaching to one congregation, we have no such luxury of anonymity. Over time, the quality of our lives will be known by our congregations. And, over time, this knowledge will either empower or undermine the effectiveness of our preaching.

In the demonstration of his sovereignty, God can and sometimes does use ungodly preachers to proclaim truth with life-changing power. However, this is not common, and the effectiveness of such "ministry" rarely seems to endure.

Ultimately, no matter how God calls one to preach, it must be understood that his call involves more than simply proclaiming his message out loud. In addition, the call to preach is a call to *be* God's message. Preaching, as modeled by Christ and defined by the New Testament, does not happen when we simply mouth God's Word. Answering God's call to preach requires proclaiming truth in such a way that it can be both heard and seen. What the preacher says can never be separated from who the preacher is. Spurgeon rightly states, "Whatever call a man may pretend to have, if he has not been called to holiness, he certainly has not been called to the ministry."[19]

3

IN VIEW OF HIS APPEARING

In the presence of God and of Christ Jesus, who will judge the living and the dead, and in view of his appearing and his kingdom, I give you this charge: Preach the Word.

2 Timothy 4:1–2a

The roar of five navy Avengers faded as they departed Fort Lauderdale Naval Air Station on a routine training flight. It was December 5, 1945. The student pilots and their leader were scheduled to fly northeast towards the Bahamas, turn south for a practice bomb run, then fly northwest to complete the triangular course that would bring them back home.

As the mission progressed, however, flight leader Lt. Charles Taylor became convinced that both his compasses had malfunctioned when he misidentified an island he wrongly assumed to be a part of the Florida Keys. Believing himself to be far southwest off course, he ordered his students to turn northeast—a course that carried them away from land and into the open waters of the Atlantic. Frustrated base personnel monitoring radio transmissions vainly tried to contact the pilots. In the end they could only listen as the leader and his students argued among themselves. Ultimately, the flight commander's order stood. With two hours of fuel remaining, the flight continued on its disastrous course. Lt. Taylor and the thirteen crewmen who followed him were never seen again.

With leadership comes a responsibility for the welfare of those who follow. In matters of importance, a leader's error, indifference, or negligence brings ruin not only to himself but also to others. Preachers carry this burden of responsibility for the spiritual welfare of their hearers. God makes this clear to his prophet Ezekiel when the Lord exhorts:

> Son of man, I have made you a watchman for the house of Israel; so hear the word I speak and give them warning from me. When I say to the wicked man, "You will surely die," and you do not warn him or speak out to dissuade him from his evil ways in order to save his life, that wicked man will die for his sin, *and I will hold you accountable for his blood*. But if you do warn the wicked man and he does not turn from his wickedness or from his evil ways, he will die for his sin; but you will have saved yourself.[1]

As a preacher, Paul recognized his accountability for the spiritual welfare of his hearers. Speaking to church leaders at the close of his ministry in Ephesus, he states, "I declare to you today that I am innocent of the blood of all men. For I have not hesitated to proclaim to you the whole will of God."[2] Paul understood that had he not fully executed his call to preach in Ephesus, he would share responsibility for the condemnation of his hearers and, along with them, be worthy of judgment.

Ezekiel and Paul remembered what we sometimes forget—for every preacher a day of accountability is coming. An evaluation will be made. Did we fully answer our call to preach? As God's spokespersons, did we withhold truth, distort truth, or hide it behind our own contradictory lives? If so, we will be held liable for whatever eternal loss results in our hearers' lives. Remembering this can't help but motivate us to *both* speak and be God's word to our congregations. Spurgeon had this in mind when he challenged preachers, "Let the awful and important thought of souls being

saved by our preaching, or left to perish and be condemned to
hell through our negligence—I say, let this awful and tremendous
thought dwell ever upon our spirits."[3]

Of course, Spurgeon's challenge is not original. It echoes Paul's
exhortation found in 2 Timothy 4:1–2:

> In the presence of God and of Christ Jesus, who will judge the liv-
> ing and the dead, and in view of his appearing and his kingdom, I
> give you this charge: Preach the Word; be prepared in season and
> out of season; correct, rebuke and encourage—with great patience
> and careful instruction.

Christ Jesus, who will judge the living and the dead, is coming to
judge preachers too. It is in view of his appearing—in view of that
day when we will give an account—the charge, "Preach the Word!"
is given. In view of Christ's coming, preach it patiently. Preach it
faithfully. Preach it appropriately in every situation. Preach it with
your lips. Preach it in your conduct.

It is often said, "We ought to serve God out of no motive
but love." Perhaps. But here Paul reminds us that love is not
the sole motivation God offers preachers. In Scripture we find
two more—the threat of judgment and the promise of reward.
Paul never hints that these motives are suspect. They are not
impure. As biblical inducements they are neither opposed to
nor inferior to love. This is why whenever we preach we must
preach in view of Christ's appearing. Faithfulness to our call
requires us to remember that at his appearing we will answer
for any negligence that leads to eternal loss in the lives of our
hearers. Only this awareness that eternal futures (including
our own) are at stake will keep us watching "both our lives and
our doctrine closely"—knowing that, if we persevere, we will
save both ourselves and our hearers.[4]

In view of Christ's appearing, to not watch our lives and our
doctrine closely is a serious matter. The apostle James warns, "Not
many of you should presume to be teachers, my brothers, because
you know that we who teach will be judged more strictly" (James
3:1).

Preachers, like all people, are sinners. But unlike all people, the sins of a preacher are subject to stricter judgment. Why? Because a teacher's sin has the capacity not only to destroy his own spiritual life, but also the lives of his hearers. Knowing that we "must all appear before the judgment seat of Christ"[5]—and there incur a stricter judgment—spurs a wise preacher towards greater personal righteousness and regular self-examination.

While the details are not fully revealed, the Bible is clear that our earthly conduct forever impacts our eternal well-being. The simple fact that we preach God's Word is no guarantee that judgment day will be for us a happy day. On the most tragic end of the spectrum will be preachers who discover that, even as they proclaimed God's grace to others, they never received it for themselves. Hell is the final destiny of some who preach truth. Jesus teaches this in Matthew 7:21–23. With his eyes fixed on the day of judgment, he warns:

> Not everyone who says to me, "Lord, Lord," will enter the kingdom of heaven, but only he who does the will of my Father who is in heaven. Many will say to me on that day, "Lord, Lord, *did we not prophesy in your name*, and in your name drive out demons and perform miracles?" Then I will tell them plainly, "I never knew you. Away from me you evildoers!"

The warning is clear. We can preach God's Word, look successful doing it, and still be condemned. Spurgeon reminds us:

> Believe it, brethren, God never saved any man for being a preacher, nor because he was an able preacher, but because he was a justified, sanctified man, and consequently faithful in his Master's work. Take heed, therefore, to yourselves first, that you be that which you persuade others to be, and believe that which you persuade them daily to believe, and have heartily entertained that Christ and Spirit which you offer to others.[6]

Presumably, most who preach God's Word do possess real saving faith. But even for preachers secure in their salvation, the reality of coming judgment should never be absent from our minds. While there is no threat of hell for those secure in Christ, any preacher who lives carelessly is in danger of forfeiting at least some of heaven's joys. Paul speaks of this in 1 Corinthians 3:10–15:

> By the grace God has given me, I laid a foundation as an expert builder, and someone else is building on it. But each one should be careful how he builds. For no one can lay any foundation other than the one already laid, which is Christ. If any man builds on this foundation using gold, silver, costly stones, wood, hay or straw, his work will be shown for what it is, because the Day will bring it to light. It will be revealed with fire, and the fire will test the quality of each man's work. If what he has built survives, he will receive his reward. If it is burned up, he will suffer loss; he himself will be saved, but only as one escaping through flames.

Many read this passage as a call to individual believers to carefully build their personal lives on the foundation of saving faith in Christ. However, the surrounding context clearly reveals that in these verses the basis for judgment is the quality of one's work in the building up of Christ's church. New Testament scholar Gordon Fee writes:

> This text has singular relevance to the contemporary church. It is neither a challenge to the individual believer to build his or her life well on the foundation of Christ, nor is it grist for theological debate. Rather, it is one of the most significant passages in the NT that warn—and encourage—those responsible for "building" the church of Christ. In the final analysis, of course, this includes all believers, but it has particular relevance, following so closely as it does vv. 5–9, to those with teaching/leadership responsibilities.[7]

As preachers, we have a special responsibility to build up Christ's church. With this responsibility comes an opportunity to store up for ourselves great reward. But any opportunity can be squandered. Ultimately, the extent and glory of our future reward, or lack thereof, will be determined by the quality of the material we use to "build up" Christ's church. When we remain true to Scripture, fully proclaiming and obeying it, we build up Christ's church with "gold, silver, and costly stones." In this case, the fruit of our ministry will survive the fire of Christ's judgment. We will receive eternal reward.

If, on the other hand, we build up Christ's church with "wood, hay, and straw"—living sloppy lives, sowing disunity, employing people-pleasing gimmicks, preaching sermons that delight but never confront—anything we "accomplish" today will be destroyed by the fire of Christ's judgment tomorrow. Nothing of eternal significance will be found in the ashes. Nothing worthy of reward will remain. In Christ, the preacher himself may be saved. But, incomprehensible as it seems, even as he enters heaven he suffers loss.

Paul himself recognized this possibility of losing out on heaven's reward. One eye fixed on future judgment provided all the motivation he needed to maintain diligence in his preaching ministry. Remembering God's promise to reward faithful servants with "a crown that lasts forever," Paul writes, "No, I beat my body and make it my slave so that after I have preached to others, *I myself will not be disqualified for the prize.*"[8]

Clearly then, God offers future judgment—primarily in the form of lost reward—as a legitimate and necessary motivation for preachers to live and preach with faithfulness and integrity. Even so, Paul's charge to preach in view of Christ's appearing is not primarily a call to focus on the threat of judgment. First and foremost, it is a charge to remember God's promise of reward. First Corinthians 9:25 tells us, "Everyone who competes in the games goes into strict training. They do it to get a crown that will not last; *but we do it to get a crown that will last forever.*" Likewise, the promise of 1 Peter 5:4 is for faithful elders: "When the Chief Shepherd appears, you will receive the crown of glory that will never fade away." It was this crown Paul rejoiced over as the day of his departure drew near. Confident in God's promise of reward, he exults:

> I have fought the good fight, I have finished the race, I have kept the faith. Now there is in store for me the crown of righteousness, which the Lord, the righteous Judge, will award me

on that day—and not only to me, but also to all who have longed for his appearing.[9]

When the cloud of death approaches, will you share Paul's joyful confidence that eternal reward awaits you? Such confidence springs only from the soil of a ministry bearing the marks of faithfulness and integrity.

The warning is real. God is serious when, through James, he advises, "Not many of you should presume to be teachers, my brothers, because you know that we who teach will be judged more strictly."[10] But never forget. The promise is just as real as the warning. To faithful preachers God pledges, "When the Chief Shepherd appears you will receive the crown of glory that will never fade away."[11]

Ultimately, preaching "in view of Christ's coming" means never forgetting that both we, and our hearers, will soon stand before the judgment seat of Christ. The day of Christ is real and coming soon! As preachers, we must be faithful to both speak and live the truth. Because on that day there is so much to lose. But more, on that day there is so much to gain.

PART 2

WHAT INTEGRITY IS

4

ABOVE REPROACH

You must come up to a much higher level than common manhood, if you mean to be a preacher.

Henry Ward Beecher, *Yale Lectures on Preaching*[1]

Pilot, turn right to a heading of 2-5-5 and bank it hard!" The evaluator behind me leaned over my shoulder intently studying the radar screen. He plotted our position on his chart. I knew I had called the turn too late. Flying four hundred feet above the Nevada desert, our B-52 lumbered out of our route's established corridor. I had just "busted" a check ride. Until I retrained and passed the next check ride, I was disqualified as an air force navigator. When snaking through a low-altitude training route, a navigator is allowed to stray no more than four miles from route centerline. How far from the centerline of righteousness does God allow a pastor to stray? How "saintly" must a preacher be to remain qualified to minister?

It's easier to make the case that preachers must possess godly character than to concretely define what godly character is. One thing is certain. God's requirement that a preacher be righteous in conduct is not a demand for perfection. Scripture is clear. In this life, perfection is impossible for us to attain. In fact, the person who claims to be sinless is sinning. The apostle John states, "If we claim to be without sin, we deceive ourselves and the truth is not in us . . . If we claim we have not sinned, we make him [God] out to be a liar and his word has no place in our lives."[2] Expressing this same truth, Solomon inquires, "Who can say, 'I have kept my heart pure; I am clean and without sin'?"[3] Ecclesiastes 7:20 adds, "There is not a righteous man on earth who does what is right and never sins."

In light of this, it is apparent that if sinless perfection is a requirement for preaching, the only one qualified is Christ himself! But if not perfection, what does God require of us before he calls us "righteous" in a practical sense? What does it mean for a preacher to be godly? Philippians 3:12–14 offers an answer. Perhaps the most godly, and effective, minister found in the pages of the New Testament is the apostle Paul. Reflecting on his own pursuit of Christlikeness, he writes:

> Not that I have already obtained all this [the full knowledge of Christ and the power of his resurrection], *or have already been made perfect*, but I press on to take hold of that for which Christ has taken hold of me. Brothers, I do not consider myself yet to have taken hold of it. But one thing I do: Forgetting what is behind and straining toward what is ahead, I press on toward the goal to win the prize for which God has called me heavenward in Christ Jesus.

The great preacher Paul was not perfect. He openly admits it. He was, however, a godly man both qualified and effective as a preacher. But if Paul wasn't perfect, how was he godly? In Paul's example we learn that practical godliness is not the attainment of perfect holiness, but the pursuit of it. A godly life is a life fully engaged in the process of spiritual growth. It is a life marked by progress in the faith. It is this progress, not perfection, that marks the integrity God requires of preachers. This is clear in Paul's instructions to Timothy:

Don't let anyone look down on you because you are young, but set
an example for the believers in speech, in life, in love, in faith and
in purity. Until I come, devote yourself to the public reading of
Scripture, to preaching and to teaching. Do not neglect your gift,
which was given you through a prophetic message when the body
of elders laid their hands on you. Be diligent in these matters; give
yourself wholly to them, *so that everyone may see your progress.*[4]

Timothy, the pastor, is called to be an example to the believers
in his congregation. But notice his example is one of progress,
not perfection! Of course there is more. The spiritual integrity
required of a pastor cannot be defined only in terms of ongoing
progress in the faith. In almost every new believer we find an example of someone making progress in his or her faith. Even so,
few claim that someone still in their spiritual infancy is biblically
qualified to pastor and preach. Paul's lists of the character qualities
required of elders (1 Tim. 3:2–7 and Titus 1:6–9) make it clear that
a believer's attitude and conduct should give evidence of an already
deep walk with Christ *before* they assume the role of pastor.

The preacher, then, is required to possess proven godly character and, at the same time, demonstrate continued progress in
the faith. Such preachers are not only mature in the faith, but also
maturing. They are able to serve as visual aides for young believers
trying to grasp what a growing Christian is. Godly pastors are those
actively learning to respond to life's circumstances God's way. When
they sin, they seek forgiveness. When sinned against, they learn to
forgive even as they have been forgiven. When grieving, they still
trust God. When suffering, they learn what God is teaching in the
midst of their pain.

When praised, they strive for humility. When they fail, they accept God's grace even as they encourage others to do the same. They
are examples—even if imperfect ones—of commitment to Christ
and his church. They are pictures—even if distorted ones—of what
it means to give, to serve, and to love. They are messengers others
can point to and honestly say, "There! That's what following Jesus
looks like!" They are servants whose lives can be safely imitated
because they themselves imitate Christ.

It is this overall pattern of Christlike living Paul has in mind when he writes, "Now the overseer must be above reproach."[5] The Greek word translated "above reproach" is *anepilēmptos*. Literally, it describes a person who cannot be apprehended or laid hold of.[6] *The Expositor's Greek Testament* speaks of "one against whom it is impossible to bring any charge of wrong doing such as could stand impartial examination."[7]

"Above reproach" best describes the overriding character trait that must mark our lives as preachers. John Calvin wrote:

> He [the elder] must not be marked by any infamy that would lessen his authority. There will be no one found among men that is free from every vice; but it is one thing to be blemished with ordinary vices, which do not hurt the reputation . . . and another thing to have a disgraceful name, or to be stained with any baseness.[8]

Perhaps Towner best sums up the idea of "above reproach" when he comments on Paul's parallel statement found in Titus 1:6 ("An elder must be blameless."). He writes:

> "Blamelessness" is more a measure of wholeness and balance than of perfection. The code examines all dimensions of life for evidence of the Spirit's influence in each part. This kind of balanced "reading" means development toward maturity is under way. And Paul felt that "whole" believers were best suited for church leadership. The code serves equally as a yardstick of maturity for all believers. Both those in leadership and those in support positions will profit from a periodic look at the reference marks it provides; it will point out areas of neglect and areas of success, *but it will always point us to maturity in the whole life.*[9]

This "maturity in the whole life" will necessarily express itself in a preacher's conduct. Jesus affirms this when he speaks of false prophets and says, "By their fruit you will recognize them. Do people pick grapes from thorn bushes, or figs from thistles? Likewise *every good tree bears good fruit*, but a bad tree bears bad fruit."[10]

If, then, conduct expresses character, what standards of conduct ought the church expect from those called to preach? It is not my purpose to inspect every variety of spiritual fruit that grows in the life of a mature believer. In the chapters that follow, however, we will consider at least some of the character qualities that ought to be present and growing in every preacher's life.

Several cautions are in order here. First, expectations legitimately flow in two directions. If the preacher is called to be God's living example of spiritual maturity, members of the congregation are called to follow that example. It is hypocritical, and worthy of judgment, to ridicule a pastor for spiritual shortcomings when one has no intention of repenting of his or her own sin. Second, it must be remembered that no pastor, or any other believer, will be found faultless. It must be said again that the evidence of spiritual maturity is not perfection. A pastor's spiritual maturity is demonstrated by the general pattern of his conduct—not by sporadic or isolated stumbles. Third, every preacher struggles with areas of weakness. Even so, no point of weakness ought to be "glaring" and no biblically required character trait of eldership ought to be entirely absent from the life of any pastor.

A close reading of the pastoral epistles reveals a substantial number of character qualities that God calls pastors to possess. Seven of these traits are considered in the chapters that follow. They are humility, contentment, fidelity to Scripture, courage, purity of life, purity of mind, and temperance. These are not offered as a comprehensive list of qualities expressing integrity. They are chosen for discussion because very often the act of pastoring brings with it temptations to compromise in one or more of these areas. If we fail to recognize and resist these temptations, our integrity will be breeched and our effectiveness as preachers will be weakened or destroyed.

In all this we must remember that our struggle to live lives consistent with the truth we preach is spiritual warfare. Ephesians 6:12 reminds us that "our struggle is not against flesh and blood, but against the powers of this dark world and against the spiritual forces of evil in the heavenly realms . . ." Against such enemies, we are helpless. That's why the following chapters must not be understood as a simple call to self-improvement. Rather, they are a call to an ever deepening dependence on God. Yes, we must strive to bear

the fruits of integrity. But God alone has the power to defeat the
world, the sin within, and the spiritual forces of evil in the heavenly realms. Here lies our hope. Because his Spirit indwells us,
we know that in our fight for personal integrity we "do not fight
like a man beating the air" (1 Cor. 9:26). By God's grace we can
grow in righteousness. And by his grace our growth will enable
our congregations to see the sermons we live even as they hear the
sermons we preach.

5

HUMILITY

For God, who thrusts out a proud angel, will not tolerate a proud preacher, either.

Richard Baxter, *The Reformed Pastor*[1]

Two songs to go and then I preach. For me the week had been marked by too little diligence and too much daydreaming. I prepared a sermon but knew I hadn't given God or my church family my best. So I did the only thing I could. I pleaded for mercy—mercy for me and for the congregation who had come expecting to be spiritually fed. One song left. I prayed harder. "Lord, somehow, bring this sermon together. Lord, please make it work!" As I preached it did come together. The rough spots smoothed out and, in a special way, God spoke through me that day. In fact, that sermon went so well I could not help but congratulate myself when it was done.

There is a legitimate satisfaction we feel when we've given our best to God and seen it blessed. On this Sunday that's not what I was feeling. I was struggling with the temptation of pride and self-glory.

Few sins attack more subtly and destroy ministry more thoroughly than unbridled pride. The destructive power of pride and God's hatred of it are clearly expressed in his Word. James 4:6 reminds us, "God opposes the proud but gives grace to the humble." If God opposes the proud, it follows that proud preachers are destined to fail.

Proverbs 16:18 warns, "Pride goes before destruction, a haughty spirit before a fall." That this warning applies to teachers of God's Word is clear when Jesus condemns proud, self-exalting Pharisees. Matthew 23:5–12 offers a case study in self-destructive pride when Jesus says:

> Everything they [the Pharisees and teachers of the law] do is done for men to see: They make their phylacteries wide and the tassels on their garments long; they love the place of honor at banquets and the most important seats in the synagogues; they love to be greeted in the marketplaces and to have men call them "Rabbi." But you are not to be called "Rabbi," for you have only one Master and you are all brothers. And do not call anyone on earth "father," for you have one Father, and he is in heaven. Nor are you to be called "teacher," for you have one Teacher, the Christ. The greatest among you will be your servant. *For whoever exalts himself will be humbled, and whoever humbles himself will be exalted.*

Pride, and the craving for recognition it leads to, threatens our ultimate standing in eternity. When we as preachers draw attention to ourselves—trying to impress our hearers with our knowledge, our "spiritual depth," and our titles—we will, in the end, receive the opposite of what we pursue. By heaven's reckoning, self-exaltation is self-humiliation. On the other hand, self-humiliation for Christ's sake brings exaltation. This is not an easy principle to live by. It requires faith. Why? Because the final exaltation of the humble won't happen in this life. Only in the age to come will the last be first and the first be last. Expositor William Barclay reminds us:

> If there is one danger which confronts the Christian teacher and preacher more than another, it is to set before himself the wrong standards of success. It can often happen that the man who has never been heard of outside his own sphere of work is in God's eyes a far greater success than the man whose name is on every lip.[2]

We must take Jesus at his word. Only when we believe that God will exalt the humble in heaven, will we stop striving to exalt ourselves as we serve him here on earth.

But not only does pride and the hunger for recognition endanger our future standing in heaven, it also threatens the eternal well-being of our congregations. As preachers, our pride endangers those who hear us because we cannot preach for our own glory without masking the glory of Christ. Few things can be more abhorrent to God than preachers who inflate their own egos by seeking followers after themselves. The only way we can draw followers after ourselves is by drawing them away from Christ. If we promote our own wisdom, we betray God's wisdom. If we trust in our own persuasive powers, we deny the power of the cross. We dare not deflect our hearers' attention away from Jesus in this way. Barclay warns:

> The Christian teacher and preacher is always faced with certain temptations. There is always the danger of self-display. There is always the temptation to demonstrate one's own cleverness and knowledge and wisdom. There is always the temptation to seek to attract notice to oneself instead of to God's message.[3]

Theologian James Denney adds, "No man can bear witness to Christ and to himself at the same time . . . no man can give at once the impression that he himself is clever and that Christ is mighty to save."[4]

Pride leads to self-promotion and self-promotion endangers Christ's church. But pride's destructive power is not only unleashed through preaching that promotes self, but also through the practice of prayerless preaching. Only humble preachers recognize their dependence on God. And only pastors who recognize their dependence on God seriously pray. Spurgeon writes:

> The minister who does not earnestly pray over his work must surely be a vain and conceited man. He acts as if he thought himself sufficient of himself, and therefore needed not to appeal to God. Yet what a baseless pride to conceive that our preaching can ever be in itself so powerful that it can turn men from their sins, and bring them to God without the working of the Holy Ghost.[5]

This presence of Holy Spirit power in preaching is sometimes called "unction." English pastor W. E. Sangster writes:

> Unction is that mystic plus in preaching which no one can define and no one (with any spiritual sensitivity at all) can mistake. Men have it, or they do not have it. It is a thing apart from good sermon outlines, helpful spiritual insights, wise understanding, or eloquent speech.
>   . . . Unction comes only of praying. Other things precious to a preacher come of prayer *and* something else. Unction comes only of praying. If nothing else revealed the poverty of our secret prayers, the absence of unction would. Able preaching can often reveal the cleverness of a man. "What clear distinctions! What dexterous use of words! What telling illustrations!" Unction reveals the presence of God.[6]

Without unction our preaching might impress people, but it can never change their lives. It is God who empowers preaching! It is God who changes lives! Do we believe it? If so, we will pray. Any preacher too proud to pray hard and pray often strips his preaching of God's power and dooms his ministry to eternal mediocrity.

As preachers, humility is critical to us. Unless humility marks our lives our preaching becomes self-promoting and prayerless. As fallen people, however, humility is not natural for us. Even when we gain a measure of it we can become proud that we're humble. One step forward in our spiritual lives easily becomes a point of temptation for pride. Cotton Mather expressed our dilemma, lamenting, "I found, that, when I met with enlargement in prayer or preaching, or answered a question readily or suitably, I was apt to applaud myself in my own mind."[7]

For preachers, pride is an occupational hazard. Pastor and scholar John Stott warns:

> Every preacher knows the insidious temptation to vainglory to which the pulpit exposes him. We stand there in a prominent position, lifted above the congregation, the focus of their gaze and the object of their attention. It is a perilous position indeed.[8]

In light of our "perilous position," how can we guard ourselves against pride? How can we fix our desires on Christ's glory instead of our own? One important key is a proper understanding of what biblical humility is. Humility is not the absence of all confidence. Rather, it is the presence of confidence rooted in its proper source. This is the humility Paul possessed. In 2 Corinthians 3:4–6, Paul defends his apostolic ministry against the claims of false teachers, writing, "Such confidence as this is ours through Christ before God. Not that we are competent in ourselves to claim anything for ourselves, but our competence comes from God. *He has made us competent as ministers* of a new covenant."

It would be hard to imagine that anyone reading Paul's letters could come to any conclusion other than that he was a confident man. Yet, at the same time he is supremely confident, he is also humble—sincerely calling himself "the least of the apostles," "less than the least of all God's people," and "the worst of sinners."[9] How is it possible for one so confident to be honestly humble at the same time? The answer is found in the source of his confidence.

In 2 Corinthians 3:4–6, Paul reveals that the confidence he possessed in his ministry was not self-confidence. This was in spite of the fact that, humanly speaking, he had every reason to be self-confident. Paul did, after all, possess a more impressive heritage, more outward righteousness, more zeal, and a better education than any of his apostolic contemporaries.[10] Even so, instead of anchoring his confidence to his worldly qualifications, Paul acknowledged his incompetence so he might possess a divine competence that only comes from God.

Humility, then, is not the absence of all confidence. It is the rejection of *self*-confidence. Humility is confidence not in what we believe ourselves capable of, but rather, confidence in what we know God is capable of through us.

Here, an important point must be made. While the "us" part of this equation is not primary, it is important. Biblical humility is not an exercise in self-depreciation. The "Aw shucks, it weren't nothin'" syndrome is nowhere to be found in Scripture. In Paul's mind his service to the Lord was in fact something—something great. In the pages of the New Testament, Paul speaks freely of his own competence (2 Cor. 3:6), his own sufferings (2 Cor. 11:24–29), and his own hard labor for Christ (1 Cor. 15:10). Paul was no robot. He chose these things for himself even as we must choose them for ourselves. That is why it is something—something great—when we too choose to develop and exercise the spiritual gifts God gives us. It is something great when we choose sacrifice over comfort for the sake of his kingdom. It is something great when we work hard in Christ's service. Humility never means denying the value of what we do. It does, however, mean keeping the things we do in proper perspective. Humility is never a claim to have done nothing. Instead, it is the realization that all we have done has been done in God's strength and by God's grace.

In the end, we are not the heroes of our own stories. God is. Left to ourselves we are run-of-the-mill sinners—helpless sinners. Apart from God all of our efforts and all of our talents have no eternal significance. Recognizing this is the soil humility grows in. Ultimately, humility means acknowledging that all glory belongs to God because every righteous thought we think, every righteous decision we make, and every righteous deed we do is nothing less than the expression of his grace at work in us. Because of this, all we do leads to God's praise and not our own. Paul says it best in 1 Corinthians 1:31, exhorting, "Let him who boasts boast in the Lord."

It is true. Every preacher loses some battles to pride. But no preacher can afford to give up the war. For all of us there is a fine line between carefully crafting a sermon for God's glory and crafting it for our own glory. Each week we should prayerfully ask ourselves if we have crossed that line. M'Cheyne pleads, "Pray for more knowledge of your own heart—of the total depravity of it—of the awful depths of corruption that are there."[11] This is not a morbid plea. Neither is it a plea to deny the value of our own labor. Rather, it is a call to remember what we are apart from God's grace. It is a call to pursue humility because, left to ourselves, we have no reason to be proud.

6

CONTENTMENT

Discontent may be said to be one of the prevailing sins of the ministerial world. How prevalent it is the public does not fully know, for
ministers who are discontented do not shout their dissatisfaction
from the house-top. They write it in bulky letters and send it in
sealed packages to their ministerial brethren.

Charles Edward Jefferson,
Quiet Hints to Growing Preachers in My Study[1]

He was a church planter just like me. His ministry in the Salt Lake
City area had begun in 1986 just like mine. As I parked in front
of his beautiful brick home with a three-car garage, I recognized
that that's where the similarities ended. I had only stopped by to
drop off the videotapes I had borrowed from his church. Even so,
I was more than happy to stay when he invited me to sit with him
in his backyard. The setting was perfect. The spring morning was
warm and the flowering trees were in full, fragrant bloom. The
glistening granite peaks of the Wasatch Range seemed to rise up
from the lush fairways of the golf course that bordered his yard. We
talked shop and compared notes. The attendance at the church he
had planted was three times that of ours. They were in the middle

of a building program (beautiful brick just like his house). They had an ideal location in a part of the valley exploding with growth. Their facility would have adequate parking. Our property boasted a total of 14 spaces. They ran two services. I was still wondering why we couldn't fill one. But I wondered more than that.

As I drove away I wondered why God was holding back on me. We had started our ministries at the same time. But we sure didn't seem to be reaping the same fruit or enjoying the same benefits. "Lord," I demanded, "why is his house nicer and his view more picturesque than mine? Why's he got a three-car garage when I have no garage at all? Why has his church grown more? Why is he more 'successful' than me?" These were ugly questions—wicked inquiries exposing a heart infected by coveting and sinful discontent.

One issue often overlooked today when character is discussed is contentment. The omission is major. There is perhaps no greater need in the North American church today than to hear contentment preached and see it modeled by its pastors. Much sin and suffering among God's people (including pastors) sprout from the root of discontent. Foolish financial decisions and enslaving debt are often the fruit of refusing to be content with God's provision. That divorce in our church which catches us by surprise is frequently only the end of a long, family-destroying process birthed by discontent in the heart of a husband or a wife.

Contentment, or lack of it, provides an important window into the state of a preacher's spiritual life. The presence of contentment expresses heart obedience to the tenth commandment, "You shall not covet your neighbor's wife. You shall not set your desire on your neighbor's house or land, his manservant or maidservant, his ox or donkey, or anything that belongs to your neighbor."[2] In other words, "You shall be content with what the Lord your God has provided *you*!"

Failure to be content in the place God puts you or with the material provision he provides is sin. But more, it is a sin that, if not quickly dealt with, will metastasize and become terminal to spiritual life. According to Romans 1:21, it is the refusal to give thanks (a mark of discontent) that leads to outright rebellion against God. Speaking of wicked men and women who suppress the truth about their Creator, Paul writes, "For although they knew God, they neither glorified him as God *nor gave thanks to him*, but their foolish hearts were darkened." In light of this truth, it is no surprise that the first step towards the fall was the sowing of discontent in Eve's heart. In Genesis 2, God graciously gave the man and the woman the fruit of every tree but one in Eden's garden. Adam and Eve moved well down the road of rebellion the moment they permitted Satan to distract them from all God had given and caused them instead to fixate on the one thing he had not.[3] It is the same for us.

The absence of contentment in the life of a preacher, then, is a serious matter. In a time when sexual sin among ministers captures so much attention, it should be remembered that the Bible classifies greed (another expression of discontent) as an equally serious sin. "For of this you can be sure: No immoral, impure *or greedy* person—such a man is an idolater—has any inheritance in the kingdom of Christ and of God."[4]

In light of this it is no surprise to discover that those who consistently choose coveting over contentment are deemed unqualified to preach. First Timothy 3:3 requires an elder be one who is "not a lover of money." Likewise, Peter pleads with elders to shepherd God's people "because you are willing, as God wants you to be; *not greedy for money*, but eager to serve."[5]

Why must preachers be people "not greedy for money"? Why must their lives be marked by contentment with God's provision? One reason has to do with how a pastor chooses his place of ministry. One night, during a stopover in Troas, the apostle Paul saw a vision of a man from Macedonia begging him to "come and help us."[6] He rightly concluded that God was calling him and his companions to preach in Macedonia. What if Paul had been "a lover of money"? Would he have queried the man in his vision about the salary package being offered? Would not a love for money have clouded Paul's thinking about whether to go or stay? As it was, he immediately obeyed God's call and—at least in the case of Thessalonica—seems to have been paid nothing of this world's goods in return for his obedience.[7]

Unlike Paul, "lovers of money" tend to determine God's place for them, at least in part, based on the compensation offered.

Ultimately, it is hurtful to both the preacher and Christ's church when a pastor leaves a place of God's calling in pursuit of a better financial package. This is not to say that no consideration ought to be given to personal finances when considering a call to a church. It is to say that money should never be the primary factor that determines where we serve.

But *where* a "lover of money" preaches is not nearly as big a concern as *what* gets preached. Those who choose coveting over contentment ultimately distort, or even contradict, God's truth. This was the case in Micah 3:5 where God condemned the preachers of Israel, saying, "As for the prophets who lead my people astray, if one feeds them, they proclaim, 'peace'; if he does not, they prepare to wage war against him." If there is any doubt concerning the motives of these prophets, verse 11 removes it. Speaking of Israel's "ministers" it reads, "Her leaders judge for a bribe, her priests teach for a price, and her prophets tell fortunes for money." Likewise, Jeremiah 6:13–14 speaks of covetous ministers, "From the least to the greatest, all are greedy for gain; prophets and priests alike, all practice deceit. They dress the wound of my people as though it were not serious. 'Peace, peace,' they say when there is no peace."

The propensity of "money lovers" to preach lies for profit is not an exclusively Old Testament phenomenon. The main motivation of the false teachers Timothy resisted in Ephesus seems to have been money. They were more than willing to preach what people wanted to hear in order to enrich themselves. Concerning such teachers Paul writes:

> If anyone teaches false doctrines and does not agree to the sound instruction of our Lord Jesus Christ and to godly teaching, he is conceited and understands nothing. He has an unhealthy interest in controversies and quarrels about words that result in envy, strife, malicious talk, evil suspicions and constant friction between men of corrupt mind, who have been robbed of the truth *and who think that godliness is a means to financial gain*.[8]

Of course the biblical examples cited above are worse case scenarios perpetrated by unbelieving enemies of God. Thankfully, most pastors of Bible-believing churches don't fit that profile. It's hard to imagine that any person truly born again and called by God preaches out of a motivation of pure greed. Even so, pastors who allow their hearts to drift out of the calm waters of contentment into the churning rapids of discontent will discover that the focus of their preaching drifts too. Discontent with one's salary can add an angry edge to preaching that betrays God's love. Pastors overly concerned about money may find themselves avoiding sermons on the dangers of riches or the sin of materialism so as not to offend the well-off givers who make the church budget work. And what happens when a lack of contentment lures a pastor deep into debt? Won't that debt hinder his ability to give freely? If so, will pastors freely preach on giving when they themselves are unable to freely give?

In a world where so few are content, God's people need pastors who are content—preachers who both proclaim and demonstrate that "a man's life does not consist in the abundance of his possessions."[9] But how? How can we resist the nonstop enticements that bombard us and stimulate our appetites to want more than we have even when we have enough? Philippians 4:11–13 offers an answer, although it is not an easy one. Having just thanked the Philippians for financially supporting him, Paul writes:

> I am not saying this because I am in need, *for I have learned to be content* whatever the circumstances. I know what it is to be in need, and I know what it is to have plenty. *I have learned the secret of being content* in any and every situation, whether well fed or hungry, whether living in plenty or in want. I can do everything through him who gives me strength.

According to Paul, contentment is a learned habit. How difficult is the lesson? So difficult that Paul says it can only be learned "through him who gives me strength." Because the corruption of our old nature remains, maintaining an attitude of contentment will never, in this life, be an effortless task. Paul suggests that contentment is a practiced discipline we choose to exercise in every situation—whether we find ourselves in times of want or times of plenty. According to Paul, contentment has nothing to do with what we have or don't have. It has everything to do with a heart that refuses to trust in or chase after things that have no bearing on our eternal well-being or usefulness to God.

In 1 Timothy 6:6–8, Paul offers two principles by which we can train our hearts to be content. He writes, "But godliness with contentment is great gain. For we brought nothing into the world, and we can take nothing out of it. But if we have food and clothing, we will be content with that." The first principle that promotes contentment is: Don't crave things you can't keep. Paul reminds us that "we brought nothing into this world, *and we can take nothing out of it.*" Anything we can't keep forever should never become a motivating force in our lives. All of us can quote Jesus' words, "Do not store up for yourselves treasures on earth, where moth and rust destroy, and where thieves break in and steal. But store up for yourselves treasures in heaven, where moth and rust do not destroy, and where thieves do not break in and steal."[10] To what extent have we taken Christ's advice? Are we more motivated by salary packages than we should be? Are we driven more by comfort or commitment? Do we pursue treasure that will not last? These are questions we ought to ask ourselves regularly.

Paul's second principle that promotes contentment is: Expect only what you need. In the work of ministry it's easy to expect far more than we really need. In fact, as pastors, it's easy for us to adopt an attitude of entitlement. This temptation can prove to be powerful for those who have worked long and hard in ministry. Jesus recognized this and reminds us of the attitude we must strive to maintain:

> Suppose one of you had a servant plowing or looking after the sheep. Would he say to the servant when he comes in from the field, "Come along now and sit down and eat"? Would he not rather say, "Prepare my supper, get yourself ready and wait on me while I eat and drink; after that you may eat and drink"? Would he thank the servant because he did what he was told to do? *So you also, when you*

have done everything you were told to do, should say, "We are unworthy servants; we have only done our duty."[11]

Many churches are becoming more aware of their responsibility to encourage and honor their pastors. In many congregations it has become common to observe October as "Pastor Appreciation Month." While this is good, these words of Jesus offer a caution. As preachers, we must never come to the place where we demand such expressions of appreciation as though we are entitled to them. Faithfulness in ministry is a preacher's duty even when the task proves to be thankless. No one exemplifies this better than Paul. It is incredible that Paul, in spite of all he suffered for Christ's sake, never reached the place in ministry where he adopted an attitude that he had "paid his dues" and was thus entitled to more money, greater privilege, special blessing, or gifts from those he served. Paul never allowed a sense of entitlement to corrupt his motivation.

That's why in 1 Timothy 6:8 Paul reminds us that, in serving Christ, God's provision of food and clothing is sufficient. Because we possess God's promise of heaven, these basics essential for life are all we ultimately need during our stay on earth. God neither owes nor promises us anything more. When we really believe this, we will not covet the things God chooses to withhold from us. Instead, we will be amazed at all God gives beyond life's essentials.

When we refuse to crave what we cannot keep and choose to expect only what we truly need, we will learn contentment like Paul learned it. A pastor so schooled is a great blessing to God's people. To the materialistic such pastors model restraint. To the unappreciative they model gratitude. To the whole church they demonstrate the freedom from materialism God offers to all.

In the end, the contented heart is the heart that trusts God. Hebrews 13:5 offers both a command and a promise. "Keep your lives free from the love of money and be content with what you have, because God has said, 'Never will I leave you; never will I forsake you.'" If we believe the promise, we'll obey the command.

7

FIDELITY TO GOD'S WORD

Although there are, strictly speaking, no prophets or apostles today,
I fear there are false prophets and false apostles. They speak their
own words instead of God's Word. Their message originates in
their own mind.

John Stott, *The Preacher's Portrait* [1]

It made me want to run outside to see if there was really a cross
on the church's steeple. Did I just hear the preacher say what I
thought I heard? Yes, the statement had been clear. In the course
of his sermon the preacher had proclaimed that the doctrine of
reincarnation is "a biblical option" Christians need to consider.
Somewhere along the way he had read a biblical text—and then
quickly departed from it. I wanted to stand up and scream, "Heretic!" Out of courtesy for those who invited me I resisted the urge.
To this day I am not certain I made the right choice.

An extreme example of a preacher departing from the truth
of Scripture? Certainly. But it should be remembered that in
God's eyes any departure by a preacher from the clear teachings of
his Word is extreme. Any substitution—subtle or not—of human

thinking for biblical truth is worthy of judgment. For this reason, our fidelity to the truth of Scripture is a critical element of our integrity. As preachers we are never free to create our own message or to derive it from any source other than Scripture. In fact, in terms of transforming lives, there is no reason to preach at all if we do not preach the Bible. On this point God is clear—only by the preaching of his Word can unbelievers come to Christ. Only by the preaching of his Word can believers grow in Christ.

Concerning the conversion of unbelievers, Paul writes:

> How, then can they call on the one they have not believed in? And how can they believe in the one of whom they have not heard? And how can they hear without someone preaching to them? . . .Consequently, *faith comes from hearing the message, and the message is heard through the word of Christ.*[2]

As preachers, we offer nothing of significance to unbelievers if we do not offer them the unaltered Word of God. But there is more. In the same way Scripture is God's instrument for salvation in the unbeliever's life, it is his instrument for spiritual growth in the lives of believers. On the night prior to his death, Jesus prayed for the disciples he was leaving behind in this world. Praying for their protection from the evil one, he pled, "Sanctify them by the truth; your word is truth."[3] According to Jesus, it is God's Word that sanctifies believers. It is proclaimed truth that molds a Christian into his likeness.

Because only the proclamation of Scripture can draw unbelievers to Christ and enable believers to become like him, we cannot be effective—as God defines effectiveness—if we do not preach God's Word exclusively. Paul confirms this when he defines his own call to preach as a call to be God's ambassador, "And he has committed to us the message of reconciliation. We are therefore Christ's ambassadors, as though God were making his appeal through us."[4] As ambassadors, we represent the one who sends us. We are never to be the originators of the message we proclaim. Instead, our calling is to relay the message God has *already* spoken.

That we must never be the originators of our message is also affirmed in Paul's portrayal of the preacher as steward. In 1 Corinthians 4:1–2, Paul again speaks of his ministry and writes, "Let a man regard us in this manner, as servants of Christ, *and stewards of the mysteries of God.* In this case, moreover, it is required of stewards that one be found trustworthy."[5] As Stott reminds us, "The steward is the trustee and dispenser of another person's goods."[6] As stewards, we do not tamper with or amend God's Word. We dispense "the goods" exactly as we have received them.

This fidelity to God's revealed truth is an obligation Paul seeks to impress on Timothy when he exhorts, "What you have heard from me, keep as the pattern of sound teaching, with faith and love in Christ Jesus. Guard the good deposit that was entrusted to you—guard it with the help of the Holy Spirit who lives in us."[7]

What does it mean for us to "guard the good deposit" entrusted to us? Again, Paul's example provides the answer. In his departing words to the Ephesian elders, Paul claims, "I am innocent of the blood of all men. For I have not hesitated to proclaim to you *the whole will of God.*"[8] Faithful preachers proclaim all of Scripture—Old Testament and New Testament, well-known passages and lesser-known passages, verses that move them deeply and verses that may not move them at all. It matters not. The whole message is entrusted to the preacher and the whole message must be relayed.

But not only did Paul faithfully proclaim God's whole message, he proclaimed it accurately. Referring again to his own faithfulness as God's ambassador and steward, the apostle writes, "We do not use deception, *nor do we distort the word of God.* On the contrary, *by setting forth the truth plainly* we commend ourselves to every man's conscience in the sight of God."[9]

Guarding the good deposit entrusted to us requires that we proclaim the whole Word of God without distortion. That's not easy. The lenses of our understanding can only be ground clear in the labor of hard study. With this in mind, Paul challenges Timothy, "Do your best to present yourself to God as one approved, a workman who does not need to be ashamed and who correctly handles the word of truth."[10]

The first call of this verse is that we be "workmen." Nineteenth-century pastor Charles Bridges reminds us, "We are to be laborers, not loiterers, in the Lord's vineyard."[11] In many churches no one keeps track of a pastor's time. The temptation towards sloth is real for those of us who are not by nature "self-starters." Yielding to such sloth in the area of sermon preparation can be easily hidden from others (and from ourselves). Lazy preachers can easily hide behind a schedule packed with administrative duties, appointments, and church busy-work. By packing our schedules this way—or allowing others to pack it for us—we avoid the hard labor of wrestling weekly with a biblical text and its application. Sermon preparation is then relegated to a few hours on Friday or Saturday with predictable results.

We can also hide our sloth behind an air of "super-spirituality." Some dismiss the hard work of study as "fleshly effort." If the preacher will only have the faith to "let go and let God," the sermon will be given at the moment of its preaching. Concerning this approach to sermon preparation, revivalist Sam Jones commented:

> I see a preacher starting out. He never looks at a book, never thinks, never studies; he is going to open his mouth and let the Lord fill it. Well, the Lord does fill a fellow's mouth as soon as he opens it, but He fills it with air. And there's many an old air-gun going through this country professing to be a preacher.[12]

As stewards, we are called to systematically dispense God's Word without distortion. This requires diligent study—week in and week out. Perhaps Puritan pastor Richard Baxter sums it up best when he challenges us, "Study hard, for the well of spiritual knowledge is deep, and our brains are shallow."[13]

But ultimately, hard work is only a means to an end. Second Timothy 2:15 not only calls us to be workmen, but workmen "*who correctly handle the word of truth.*" The goal of the hard work of study is not just to produce a sermon, but a sermon that accurately reflects the message of the passage we're preaching. It's not enough for us to speak truth. We must strive to preach the specific truth actually found in our chosen text. This can be a challenge. Studying a biblical text under the pressure of Sunday's sermon deadline presents many temptations, and no preacher successfully resists them all. In a 1979 survey conducted by Raymond McLaughlin, three-quarters of the pastors responding admitted that they were sometimes guilty of "reading into the text" as they prepared sermons. More than a third admitted to "violating the context" of their sermon text at least some of the time. And almost two-thirds admitted that they sometimes forced a biblical text to fit their sermon idea rather than making the sermon idea fit the text.[14]

We must come to terms with the reality that these practices, especially when intentional, are sin. This is easy for us to recognize when those guilty are members of nonorthodox groups. Mormon missionaries often claim that Ezekiel 37:15–17 prophesies the coming of the *Book of Mormon*. The passage reads:

> The word of the LORD came to me: "Son of man, take a stick of wood and write on it, 'Belonging to Judah and the Israelites associated with him.' Then take another stick of wood, and write on it, 'Ephraim's stick, belonging to Joseph and all the house of Israel associated with him.' Join them together into one stick so that they will become one in your hand."

Mormon exegesis defines the stick of wood "belonging to Judah" as the Bible and "Ephraim's stick, belonging to Joseph" as the Book of Mormon. When the Mormon missionaries explain it their way, it sounds feasible. It sounds feasible, that is, until you read the surrounding context of the passage. In verses 18–23, God himself explains that one stick represents the nation of Judah and the other the nation of Israel. In its context, the prophecy of Ezekiel 37:15–17 is nothing more, or less, than a promise that one day God would again make the two nations one. Ezekiel says nothing about the coming of the *Book of Mormon*.

As Christians, we rightly condemn Mormon "expositors" for their blatant abuse of God's Word. But are Latter-day Saints any more worthy of condemnation for their abuse of Scripture than "Bible-believing" preachers when we do the same? Is it really more legitimate to rip a verse out of its context to "prove" that rock music is evil than it is to "prove" that the *Book of Mormon* is true? Is it right to transform biblical warnings against drunkenness into absolute prohibitions against alcohol? Is God pleased when preachers read their own belief about "speaking in tongues" into a text so they can demonstrate that their personal position is the only defensible view? Should Matthew 18:19–20 be preached as a sermon on prayer when church discipline, not prayer, is the subject of its context? Whenever we abuse a biblical text, don't we corrupt the "good deposit" instead of guard it? Yes, our calling is to speak God's Word *to* the congregation. But more, our calling is to model the honest handling of God's Word *for* the congregation. Only when we submit our preconceived notions and opinions to the text can we be faithful to that call.

As preachers we are ambassadors. We are sent to proclaim a message not our own. As preachers we are stewards. We guard the message entrusted to us even as we dispense it to our hearers. This message we proclaim and guard is God's message to all humanity. Fidelity to God's Word means studying hard to understand it. Fidelity means studying humbly so we don't distort it.

8

COURAGE

. . . the temporizing spirit, that aims to please both God and man,
will meet with disappointment from both.

Charles Bridges, *The Christian Ministry*[1]

I studied the map as we headed east out of Sacramento, putting
Mather Air Force Base in our rearview mirror. On this rare day
off we, and the rest of our navigator training class, could forget
about charts, plotters, sextants, and compasses. My friend Dan
and I had decided to head for the Sierras to engage in some serious hiking. For a week, Dan, an unbeliever, had been the object
of my prayers. "Lord, as we hike, open up a clear opportunity for
me to share Christ with Dan." We parked the car at the trailhead
and began to climb the switchbacks through the trees. Several hours
later when the trail ended, we scrambled up a rock field until, finally, we reached the top. It was on that mountain peak that God
answered my prayer in a powerful way. As we ate granola, emptied
our canteens, and gazed at the hazy valley below, Dan began to talk.
As he spoke he wondered out loud about the end of the world. He

looked at me and said, "I've been reading the book of Revelation. It's scary. Do you think the world will end the way it says?"

Here it was! The opportunity I had prayed for. God hadn't just opened a door for me to share Christ, he'd knocked down the whole wall. I wish I could report that I shared the truth with Dan that day. I wish I could say that I knelt with him on that mountaintop and led him in a prayer to receive Christ as his Savior. I can't. In spite of the fact that this was the moment I had both prayed and planned for, nothing came out of my mouth. My heart raced, my stomach sank, a giant lump formed in my throat—but God forgive me—nothing came out of my mouth. I was a coward. In that moment I was afraid of what he might think of me. I feared the loss of my reputation more than I feared the loss of his soul. Almost thirty years have passed since that day Dan and I sat on a mountaintop together. Even so, I still long to have that day back—to live it over and, this time, speak boldly about Christ and his love.

Proclaiming Christ and the truths of God's Word requires courage. This is true in the ministry of personal evangelism and it is true in the ministry of preaching. Those desiring to speak God's Word without compromise face a problem. Very often, people (including God's people) don't want to hear it—at least not all of it. Most people enjoy being comforted by Scripture. Far fewer are happily confronted by it. The Bible itself gives ample evidence of this evil human tendency. When the prophet Isaiah confronted Israel with their sins and with God's coming judgment, they corporately plugged their ears. Through the prophet, God condemns them, saying:

> These are rebellious people, deceitful children, children unwilling to listen to the LORD's instruction. They say to the seers, "See no more visions!" and to the prophets, "Give us no more visions of what is right! Tell us pleasant things, prophesy illusions. Leave this way, get off this path, and stop confronting us with the Holy One of Israel!"[2]

Speaking of Israel's determination to hear only pleasant preaching, the prophet Micah proclaims, "If a liar and deceiver comes and says, 'I will prophesy for you plenty of wine and beer,' he would be just the prophet for this people!'"[3]

This bent to choose lies over unwelcome truth is not restricted to ancient Israel. That this is the normal tendency of fallen humanity is also made clear in 2 Timothy 4:3–4 where Paul warns, "For the time will come when men will not put up with sound doctrine. Instead, to suit their own desires, they will gather around them a great number of teachers to say what their itching ears want to hear."

Because people want to hear only pleasant things it is tempting for the pastor to preach only pleasant things. Why preach about hell when the Bible says so much about heaven? Why speak of judgment when we can speak of grace? Why delve into the darkness of human depravity when we can talk about God's love? Why? Because, in the end, half the truth is no truth at all. Every congregation needs to hear the whole truth, and preaching it requires courage.

When as much as half the congregation shares a background of divorce and remarriage, it requires courage to preach Jesus' words calling that practice adultery. When the well-off man sitting second row left offers you regular use of his vacation cabin—and always gives you a generous Christmas gift—an unflinching sermon on the evils of materialism becomes hard to deliver. When looking into the eyes of parents recently wounded by the revelation that their son is gay, it seems permissible to avoid the topic of homosexuality altogether. In the end, however, it is not permissible for a pastor to exclude or soften biblical truth because of the circumstances of those who hear. The preaching of any pastor who regularly yields to such temptation is rendered impotent. Reflecting on how our lack of courage plays out in the pulpit, Charles Bridges wrote:

> Subjects uncongenial to the taste and habits of influential men in our congregation are passed by, or held back from their just and offensive prominence, or touched with the tenderest scrupulosity, or expanded with wide and undefined generalities; so that the sermons (like letters put into the post-office without a direction) are addressed to no one. No one owns them. No one feels any personal interest in their contents. Thus a minister under this deteriorating influence chiefly deals in general truths devoid of

particular application—more in what is pleasing than what is direct and useful. Many other subjects may be equally necessary, or indeed more important; but these are more conciliating. There is a continual conflict between conscience and the world—"I ought to speak for conscience' sake; but I dare not speak, for fear of the world." The offensive truth must be smoothed, disguised, and intermixed, until it is attenuated into an insipid, pointless, and inoperative statement.[4]

It would be hard to imagine meeting a preacher today who has not experienced this conflict "between conscience and the world" Bridges speaks of. It seems certain that most, if not all, of us struggle at times to find the courage faithfulness requires. In McLaughlin's 1979 survey of pastors, half of those responding admitted that they sometimes preached what their people wanted to hear instead of what they needed to hear. Two out of three pastors responding admitted to avoiding unpleasant, controversial, or troublesome subjects.[5] McLaughlin comments:

> It would seem that one of the more serious ethical problems facing today's ministers is that of confronting the audience with their needs more than their desires. Today's ministers need to strengthen their prophetic roles. Whether or not parishioners "enjoy" sermons on unpleasant, controversial, or troublesome subjects, they may need such confrontation much more than they need the latest ecclesiastical jokes, magical tricks, or other forms of entertainment.[6]

The struggle to courageously preach the whole truth of God is not new. When God called Moses to be his spokesman, he stirred God's anger with a string of excuses.[7] At Jeremiah's call, God found it necessary to instruct the prophet not to be afraid of those to whom he would prophesy.[8] In 2 Timothy 1, Paul reminds his coworker that "God did not give us a spirit of timidity" and warns him several times not to be ashamed. Paul himself was more than once strengthened by a vision of Christ exhorting him, "Do not be afraid."[9]

If the struggle for courage is common, where do we find victory? Just as an end table requires three legs to stand, so Scripture offers three legs that undergird courageous preaching in our own lives and ministries. The first is the fear of God. Godly courage is not a total absence of fear. Courageous preaching is rooted in the fear of God. The preaching ministry of Isaiah was not well received in Israel. What was the source of the courage that steadied Isaiah's prophetic voice through decades of opposition? The prophet himself tells us:

> The LORD spoke to me with his strong hand upon me, warning me not to follow the way of this people. He said, "Do not call conspiracy everything that these people call conspiracy; do not fear what they fear, and do not dread it. The LORD Almighty is the one you are to regard as holy, *he is the one you are to fear, he is the one you are to dread.*"

Isaiah 8:11–12

It was Isaiah's fear of God that made him bold before men. Likewise, when Jesus sent his disciples on a preaching mission, he warned them, "Do not be afraid of those who kill the body but cannot kill the soul. Rather, *be afraid* of the One who can destroy both soul and body in hell."[10] It is sobering to note that on the last day the cowardly are condemned along with other unrepentant sinners. Revelation 21:8 reads, "But *the cowardly*, the unbelieving, the vile, the murderers, the sexually immoral, those who practice magic arts, the idolaters and all liars—their place will be in the fiery lake of burning sulfur." For preachers, a proper fear of God is a necessary foundation upon which courageous preaching is built. As Charles Bridges states, "The fear of God will subjugate the fear of man."[11]

The fear of God, of course, is not the only leg that undergirds a preacher's courage. For many pastors a stronger foundation for boldness is their trust in him. This trust grows deep in our lives when we recognize all that God has done for us in Christ. This is the experience Paul describes when he exhorts Timothy to be bold:

So do not be ashamed to testify about our Lord, or ashamed of
me his prisoner. But join with me in suffering for the gospel,
by the power of God, who has saved us and called us to a holy
life—not because of anything we have done but because of his own
purpose and grace. This grace was given us in Christ Jesus before
the beginning of time, but it has now been revealed through the
appearing of our Savior, Christ Jesus, who has destroyed death
and has brought life and immortality to light through the gospel.
And of this gospel I was appointed a herald and an apostle and a
teacher. That is why I am suffering as I am. *Yet I am not ashamed, because
I know whom I have believed, and am convinced that he is able to guard what I have
entrusted to him for that day.*[12]

Paul was a courageous herald of the gospel because he deeply
trusted God. Paul deeply trusted God because he understood what
the Lord had already done for him—destroyed the death he deserved
and replaced it with life and immortality through the gospel. Paul's
thought seems to be, "Who better to be courageous for than the
one who gives grace? Who better to trust with your life than the one
who destroys death?" Paul's example reminds us, preachers who
know God trust him. Preachers who trust God are bold.

Two legs, however, are not enough for a table to stand. The third
leg upon which our courage must rest is a hunger for God's approval. One of the detriments to courageous preaching is the desire
to please people. John reminds us that it was this desire that kept
many from publicly professing Christ in Jerusalem. John 12:42–43
states, "Yet at the same time many even among the leaders believed
in him. But because of the Pharisees they would not confess their
faith for fear they would be put out of the synagogue; *for they loved
praise from men more than praise from God.*" A preacher can ill afford to
nurture this love of man's praise. Again, it is Paul who reminds
us that courageous preaching grows out of a desire to please God
more than people. After boldly rebuking the Galatians for their
doctrinal errors he asks, "Am I now trying to win the approval
of men, or of God? Or am I trying to please men? If I were still
trying to please men, I would not be a servant of Christ."[13] To the
Thessalonians he adds, "We speak as men approved by God to be

entrusted with the gospel. *We are not trying to please men but God*, who tests our hearts."[14] Courageous preaching happens when we remember that our primary audience is ultimately an audience of One.

But even when we fear God, trust God, and seek to please God, we must take care that the resulting boldness is a boldness that honors him. God's call for courageous preaching comes with a caution. It seems that some preachers mistake crass self-righteousness for boldness. Arrogant condemnation of sin is not the same thing as spiritual boldness. Godly courage never negates love. Helping a congregation grow up in Christ requires us to "speak the truth *in love*"[15] not deliver it with the destructive blows of a verbal hammer. Along with the call for courage we need to hear M'Cheyne's call for patient love:

> Now such ought ministers be. Above all men we need "love that suffers long and is kind." Sometimes, when sinners are obstinate and hard-hearted, we are tempted to give up in despair, or to lose our temper and scold them, like the disciples calling down fire from heaven. But, brethren, we must be of another spirit. The wrath of man worketh not the righteousness of God. Only be filled with the Spirit of Christ, and it will make us patient toward all.[16]

While it is true that all preaching must be courageous, we must always remember that all courageous preaching must be tempered with love.

Sometimes, even today, when I step onto the platform, my heart races, my stomach sinks, and that lump begins to form again in my throat. I am afraid of what the congregation will think of me. I fear how they might respond to some hard or seemingly hurtful truth. In those moments I must ask myself: Do I fear God? Do I trust him? Is he the one I hunger to please? In those moments I must speak courageously—because if I will not speak courageously, I cannot speak faithfully.

9

PURITY OF LIFE

Left unbridled, the sexual misconduct perpetrated by pastors will leave the faithful disillusioned and the skepticism of critics confirmed. It will stop the ears, dull the conscience, silence the Spirit, and from the human perspective make the death of Christ irrelevant. We dare not allow this to happen!

Stanley Grenz and Roy Bell, *Betrayal of Trust*[1]

The discovery of the papyrus has rocked the world of biblical archeology. Dating from somewhere between AD 70 and 90, its preservation has been declared to be nothing short of miraculous. One by one, reluctant scholars are arriving at a common conclusion—this papyrus is indeed a newly discovered letter from the pen of the apostle Paul. Tentatively dubbed *Second Titus*, it reads:

Paul, an apostle of Christ Jesus by the will of God who saves us by his grace, to Titus my true son in the faith: Grace, mercy and peace from God and from Christ Jesus who, having paid our debt on the cross, now offers forgiveness to all willing to receive it.

When I charged you to be morally pure I did not mean that a one-time stumble into sexual sin would disqualify you from ministry. I warned you that Cretan women are enticing. You should have taken care. Titus, your sin is real. But, so is your repentance. Take heart. Your sin is forgiven—covered by Christ's blood. You are clean in God's eyes.

In spirit I am there with you. It is my decision that you must be restored to your office. Grace requires it. Besides, your gifts must not be wasted. Get back in the race! Continue to teach the young men to be pure and to live self-controlled lives. Remind those who snicker or sneer that, as a wounded healer, you are better able to understand their weaknesses as you call them to live holy lives.

On my next visit I will deal with those who oppose your restoration to ministry. The grace of the Lord Jesus Christ be with your spirit.

You're not buying this are you? And I suspect your rejection of Paul's "newly discovered" epistle is due to more than your belief in a closed canon. For most of us, it's simply not believable that Paul would write these words to a minister recently found guilty of sexual sin.

Few sins possess more potential to destroy a preacher's reputation—and the reputation of Christ—than sexual sin. The biblical demand for a pastor's moral purity seems hardly debatable. Paul makes it clear that sexual sin should never be found in any believer's life. In the last half of 1 Corinthians 6:13, he instructs, "The body is not meant for sexual immorality, but for the Lord, and the Lord for the body." In verses 18–20, he continues, "Flee from sexual immorality. All other sins a man commits are outside his body, but he who sins sexually sins against his own body . . . You are not your own; you were bought at a price. Therefore honor God with your body." Likewise, Ephesians 5:3 exhorts believers, "But *among you there must not be even a hint of sexual immorality*, or of any kind of impurity, or of greed, because these are improper for God's holy people."

Since Scripture requires moral purity of all believers, it is not surprising that pastors are called to model this purity in their own lives. In both 1 Timothy 3:2 and Titus 1:6, Paul states that an elder must be "the husband of but one wife." While this statement is often interpreted as an admonition against polygamy or divorce and remarriage, pastor and author Gene Getz sees it as a more general call to sexual purity. His understanding seems to best fit the historical context of Paul's day. According to Getz, in New Testament times it was common for affluent men to have at least three women in their lives. One woman might be a slave girl living in the house. A second might be a pagan temple prostitute. The third woman would be his wife. All three were sexually available to him. Getz writes:

> This is the kind of culture in which the apostle Paul preached the gospel.
> And it was in this kind of culture that men came to Christ. And for the first time in their lives, these new Christians heard God's message regarding moral purity: God's plan for them was to have only one woman in their lives—their wives.
> . . . Get the picture? Paul was concerned that a man who did not have victory over sexual immorality should never be appointed as a spiritual leader in the church. Therefore, Paul told Timothy that a spiritual leader must be "the husband of one wife"—or more literally, "a man of one woman."[2]

Paul's concern that all who preach be morally pure is also revealed in his direct statements to Timothy. In 1 Timothy 4:12, Paul exhorts the young pastor to "set an example for the believers in life, in love, in faith, *and in purity*." Even more direct is Paul's command for Timothy to "flee the evil desires of youth."[3]

In light of this clear biblical mandate that pastors be morally pure, it is distressing to read surveys that reveal almost 1 in 5 pastors admit to engaging in inappropriate sexual contact with women while in ministry. When *Leadership Journal* queried pastors in 1988, 18 percent admitted to having had intercourse or "other forms of sexual contact" with someone other than their spouse while in ministry. "Other forms of sexual contact" was defined as passionate kissing or fondling/mutual masturbation.[4] If these numbers reflect present reality, a critical issue confronts the church. In light of Scripture's demand for moral purity, how should pastors found guilty of sexual sin be disciplined? If removed from the pulpit, should they be allowed to return? If so, when?

These questions are not simple. God's grace must be considered along with his holiness. The good of the church must be balanced against that of the "fallen" preacher. Additionally, the legitimacy of restoring pastors guilty of immorality may vary from case to case. Should the pastor who stumbles once into sexual sin be treated the same as one involved in a long-term affair? Considering the complexity of the question, it is no surprise that disagreements exist concerning how churches should respond to a pastor's moral failure.

One common response to the moral failure of preachers is to remove them from their office for a designated period of time with the stated intent of restoring them to ministry. During this time, the offending preacher is answerable to another pastor or an accountability group. Once it is determined that the disciplined pastor has demonstrated sufficient repentance, he is permitted to return to the pulpit. Such restoration has been known to take place after an absence from active ministry as brief as six months. Perhaps, in certain circumstances, this condensed process of removal from the pulpit and restoration back into the pulpit is valid. In general, however, it appears to ignore the biblical qualifications for eldership on several counts.

As already seen, Scripture's requirement that an elder be "the husband of but one wife" is a call for moral purity. Taken at face value, a pastor recently found guilty of sexual sin does not meet this qualification. But there is more. Scripture also requires elders to be "above reproach" and to "have a good reputation with outsiders."[5] It is particularly this issue of reputation that is too often ignored when fallen preachers are quickly restored to their pulpits.

There is no question that a pastor guilty of sexual sin can quickly repent and take steps to guard against repeated sin. If this is all Scripture requires of adulterous pastors prior to their restoration, then clearly it's proper to quickly return such men to their pulpits. However, if we take the biblical demand that an elder be "above reproach" and "have a good reputation" as something more than a suggestion, restoration can be neither simple nor quick.

This requirement that a preacher be "above reproach" and that he "have a good reputation with outsiders" is the requirement that he be credible. Can any preacher recently found guilty of sexual sin be truly credible in the eyes of his congregation and community? Stanley Grenz and Roy Bell, professors at Carey/Regent College, rightly question the possibility:

> Each act of clergy indiscretion marks a violation of the Christian message and its credibility. A pastor who enters into an illicit sexual relationship reinforces the disbelief, even cynicism, of the unbelieving world. Skeptics correctly wonder how a Christian leader can honestly commend the gospel to others when his own conduct displays no higher standard of sexual morality than that of those he sees as needing the salvation message.[6]

In cases of moral failure, a legitimate return to the pulpit requires more than simple repentance—even when that repentance is sincere. Credibility as God's spokesperson must be regained. A reputation for holiness must be rebuilt. Unfortunately, in the aftermath of sexual sin, repairing a reputation takes far more time than repentance does. This being true, the practice of quickly restoring pastors guilty of sexual sin must be questioned. Spurgeon did exactly that more than a century ago:

> I hold very stern opinions with regard to Christian men who have fallen into gross sin; I rejoice that they may be truly converted, and may be with mingled hope and caution received into the church; but I question, gravely question whether a man who has grossly sinned should be very readily restored to the pulpit. As John Angell James remarks, "When a preacher of righteousness has stood in the way of sinners, he should never again open his lips in the great congregation *until his repentance is as notorious as his sin*" (emphasis mine).[7]

If we accept that *both* repentance and the repair of reputation must occur before a pastor guilty of sexual sin returns to the pulpit, it follows that any legitimate restoration process will necessarily be long. Instead of removing a pastor from active ministry for periods of one or two years, a time frame of a decade or more may be needed to honestly observe the fruits of a preacher's repentance and to reestablish his reputation as one whose life can be safely imitated. Just as important, would not this longer process of restoration make the seriousness of sexual sin more evident and the preaching of truth more credible?

But where in all this is grace for the repentant preacher? To answer, we must make a distinction between restoring a pastor *to fellowship* and restoring him *to spiritual leadership*. Scripture demands forgiveness and restoration to fellowship immediately upon repentance. Any believer, including a pastor, who repents of sin must be embraced, encouraged, and strengthened by the congregation. However, once restored to fellowship in the church, there is no biblical mandate demanding that a fallen leader be restored to office. In fact, Scripture prohibits such a move until the fallen leader demonstrates, over time, that he again qualifies for eldership according to all the standards of 1 Timothy 3:2–7.

But again the question arises, "What about grace?" One thing is certain. Quickly restoring pastors guilty of sexual sin to their pulpits has nothing to do with grace. Under the shadow of sexual sin, caution, not haste, is grace—grace for the church, grace for the disciplined pastor. Hastily restoring preachers to active ministry before they are again proven only increases the likelihood of another fall into sin. For the restored preacher this disaster certainly would bring permanent disqualification from ministry and the "stricter judgment" James 3:1 warns of. Worse, for Christ and his church, still more credibility would be lost and more lives destroyed. This is not grace. It is recklessness!

Sexual sin in the life of a preacher is far more serious than we often treat it. Still, we must remember, it is not the unpardonable sin. Again, it must be said—those guilty of sexual sin must be forgiven and, at the moment of repentance, joyfully received and restored into the full fellowship of Christ's church. Restoration to the pulpit, however, is a different matter. No preacher guilty of sexual sin should be quickly restored to his office. Sufficient time must pass until he is again known as one who is "above reproach" and one who "has a good reputation with outsiders."

As pastors, our knowledge of the power of sexual temptation—and of the consequences of yielding to it—must shape the way we do ministry. Male pastors must exercise great caution when working with and ministering to women in the church. In fact, Paul strongly implies that an ongoing ministry of personal discipleship with young women is not a ministry male pastors should undertake. We discover this when Paul instructs Titus concerning his ministry to various groups within the church. In every case but one, Paul tells Titus to interact directly with those he ministers to. That one exception involves ministry to young women. In Titus 2:1–10, Paul exhorts Titus to teach the older men; encourage the young men; teach slaves; and teach the older women. However, when the issue of training young women is addressed, Paul appoints the older women in the church to carry out this ministry. It seems likely that Paul's reason for this was to protect Titus from sexual temptation. If this made sense for Titus in his day, it certainly makes sense for us in ours. Training older women to mentor the younger women in our churches may be the most effective safeguard against sexual sin we can adopt.

Even after establishing reasonable precautions, however, it must be remembered that in a culture characterized by low standards of morality, sexual temptation remains a fact of life. The pastor who most successfully resists these temptations is the one who stays close to God and at the same time makes himself accountable to another pastor, mentor, or a group of men he can trust. The pastor who refuses to submit himself to such accountability may be flirting with moral disaster and the betrayal of his call. When sexual temptation is in view, it is critical for all preachers to heed Paul's warning, "So, if you think you are standing firm, be careful that you don't fall!"[8]

10

PURITY OF MIND

Finally, brothers, whatever is true, whatever is noble, whatever is right, whatever is pure, whatever is lovely, whatever is admirable—if anything is excellent or praiseworthy—think about such things.

Philippians 4:8

I heard what he said. The problem for me was comprehending it. From across his kitchen table the young man told me, "I have not had sex with my wife in more than a year and a half." For me, this was a foreign concept. But then, still being young in the ministry, I had not yet encountered anyone addicted to pornography. Enticed by fantasy women who don't really exist, my friend had traded the effort that true intimacy requires for masturbation with airbrushed Internet images. How tragic for any man. How much more tragic if that man is a pastor.

Moral purity is more than an issue of what we do with our bodies. It is an issue of how we choose to think and what we choose to see. Jesus teaches this in Matthew 5:27–28, "You have heard that it was said, 'Do not commit adultery.' But I tell you that anyone who looks at a woman lustfully has already committed adultery with her in his heart."

As it stands alone, the Greek word for "lust" (*epithymia*) is a neutral term. It can be used to refer to any strong desire—even the desire to be a pastor (1 Tim. 3:1). However, Jesus' use of the word in Matthew 5:28 is clearly negative. While sexual desire is both legitimate and natural, it becomes sin when misdirected. Today, such misdirected sexual lust and mental adultery are a simple mouse click away. For many preachers it's too simple. Too easy. Too enticing to resist. The end result is personal disaster. But it's more. As with any breech of a pastor's integrity, the end result of yielding to sexual fantasy or pornography is powerless preaching and famished congregations.

The battle for purity of mind is a battle we cannot afford to lose. Yet far too many of us are losing. In 1988, *Leadership Journal* surveyed their readers concerning their fantasy life. Six percent of responding pastors admitted to fantasizing daily about sex with someone other than their spouse. Twenty percent said they entertained such fantasies weekly. Thirty-five percent admitted to fantasizing about adulterous sex monthly or a few times a year. More disturbing still is the fact that 39 percent of those engaging in such fantasy believed the practice to be "harmless." In light of Jesus' warning in Matthew 5, calling such sexual fantasy "harmless" is biblically indefensible.

The temptation to lust is a reality for us all. In our war against lust we all lose some battles along the way. But losing an occasional battle to lust is entirely different from willing capitulation to sinful fantasy by calling it harmless. Grenz and Bell remind us that such fantasy is anything but harmless:

> No pastor can provide room and board for a sexual fantasy without eventually discovering that his fantasy life has undermined his biblical convictions and values first in his imagination and eventually in his behavior. Unbiblical fantasy opens the door to self-indulgence, robs the pastor of healthy sexual enjoyment, and can begin the process that leads him into sexual misconduct with all its attendant disasters.[1]

For many, the use of pornography goes hand in hand with immoral sexual fantasy. Too many preachers are yielding to pornography's lure. In 2001, *Leadership* surveyed pastors concerning their use of Internet pornography. Thirty-six percent of responding pastors admitted to visiting a pornographic website during the past year (9 percent once, 21 percent a few times during the year, 6 percent two times a month or more).[2] A 2002 survey conducted by *Pastors.com* provided results even more disturbing. In this survey, 55 percent of responding pastors admitted to visiting a pornographic website during the past year. Thirty percent of the respondents had visited a pornographic website during the previous thirty days.

It has been said that, due to a sense of isolation and on-the-job emotional stress, many pastors are especially susceptible to pornography's temptation. This may be true. Still, it's critical that we not let susceptibility become an excuse. For each of us, and for the congregations entrusted to us, there is too much at stake—and let us never forget, those stakes are eternal. As preachers of God's truth we must say no to pornography and we must say no absolutely!

If you are a pastor dabbling with Internet pornography, stop now! There are steps we can all take in our battle with the lure of pornography. *Leadership* offers these suggestions: keep your computer in a room where the door can't be locked; place your computer so the screen faces the door, don't work on your computer after your family has gone to bed.[3] In addition to this, make yourself accountable to a friend or another pastor you can trust. Purchase software that blocks pornographic websites. If need be, cancel your subscription to the Internet.

But what if it's become more than dabbling for you? What if you can't quit? Then step aside. Step aside and get professional help.[4] Step aside until you have quit. I don't say this out of a condemning spirit. I say it because from eternity's viewpoint it's better for you and it's better for the congregation you serve.

Resignation or a sabbatical from the pulpit is better for you because it delivers you from the sin of hypocrisy. Can a pastor continue to preach purity on Sundays while immersing himself in moral garbage on Mondays? We need to remember that Jesus saved his harshest words not for prostitutes, swindlers, and tax collectors (and, today, I suspect not for those caught in pornography's snare), but for hypocritical teachers of God's Word. Again, we must remember the warning of James that teachers will be judged more strictly. The pastor who steps aside because of a pornography habit spares himself the harsher judgment hypocrisy brings. But he does more than that. By stepping aside, a pastor humbles himself. And it is exactly this state of humility that is necessary before God can deliver us from the sin that enslaves.

But not only should the pastor caught in pornography's web step aside for his own sake—he should remove himself from the pulpit for the sake of the congregation he serves. Like it or not, a congregation's potential for spiritual growth is directly related to the spiritual health of its leaders. All believers, including pastors, struggle with sin. That struggle, in and of itself, certainly does not disqualify a person from ministry. However, when a preacher's life becomes consumed by any sin to the point of "addiction," he loses the moral ground required to confront sin in others. Jesus is clear on this issue:

> Why do you look at the speck of sawdust in your brother's eye and pay no attention to the plank in your own eye? How can you say to your brother, "Brother, let me take the speck out of your eye," when you yourself fail to see the plank in your own eye? You hypocrite, *first take the plank out of your own eye*, and then you will see clearly to remove the speck from your brother's eye.
>
> Luke 6:41–42

The call for a pastor caught in pornography's web to relinquish his pulpit is a call to take the time needed to "remove the plank" from his own eye. Only when he first deals with his own sin can a pastor address sin in the congregation. And only when he can address sin in the congregation does that congregation have a chance to corporately mature in Christ. The pastor who remains in office in spite of a sinful obsession endangers the spiritual well-being of the people he leads and claims to love. Jesus asks, "Can a blind man lead a blind man? *Will they not both fall into a pit? A student is not above his*

teacher, but everyone who is fully trained will be like his teacher."[5]
How can a pastor lead others to the grace that frees from addictive
sin if he has never found the way himself?

If you are a pastor who has yielded to the sin of sexual fantasy
and/or pornography, be courageous. For your own sake and the
sake of those you serve, humble yourself. If you can't stop, then
step aside from ministry and get help. Ralph Earle, founder of
Psychological Counseling Services, reminds us, "The good news
is recovery is possible. The bad news is it takes work."[6] Ultimately
that work is the work God wants to do in you. Submit yourself to
God and to those he brings into your life to help you.

Of course, the best defense against immoral fantasy and pornography is a good offense. That's why Paul exhorts, "Finally, brothers,
whatever is true, whatever is noble, whatever is right, whatever is
pure, whatever is lovely, whatever is admirable—if anything is excellent or praiseworthy—think about such things." Right thinking
pushes sinful thoughts out the door. When we read, memorize,
and meditate on Scripture, it is doubtful pornography will find a
solid foothold in our lives.

Beyond this, we must embrace life and ministry for what it is. At
times, ministry does inflict disappointment, loneliness, and pain.
We can't avoid these wounds, but we can choose how we respond to
them. Today, too many pastors seek to anesthetize disappointment
and pain with the temporary—and vacant—buzz pornography provides. Instead, we must choose to labor for real intimacy with God
and real intimacy with our wives. This choice alone demonstrates
the integrity required to preach God's Word with life-changing
power.

11

TEMPERANCE

Resolved: to maintain the strictest temperance in eating and drinking.

Jonathan Edwards, "Memoirs of Jonathan Edwards"[1]

They'll know we are Christians by our love—and by our bulging waistlines. And the larger the middle, the more likely you are to be pastor of a church." So begins a recent magazine article.[2] The article goes on to quote from a 1998 Purdue University study that found a significant correlation between being religious and being overweight. Members of evangelical denominations (especially pastors) topped the list. These findings would come as no surprise to a friend of mine who often speaks at pastors' conferences. After returning from one such event, he remarked, "I think 60 percent of the pastors there were at least twenty-five pounds overweight." Likewise, fitness guru Dr. Kenneth Cooper declares, "As a profession, pastors are the most poorly conditioned people who come through our clinic."[3]

The word "temperance" usually brings to mind the idea of restraint in the use of alcohol. In the New Testament, however, the Greek word for "temperance" (*nephalion*) generally carries a broader meaning. This is certainly true in 1 Timothy 3:2 where Paul states that an elder must be "temperate."[4] In this context, Warren Wiersbe defines *nephalion* as "well-balanced."[5] Robert C. Anderson explains, "The Greek word here means to be strong in a thing and self-controlled, especially in the area of appetites. The key thought here is moderation. We are to avoid excesses whether those excesses consist of observing inordinately long work hours or practicing gluttony in our eating habits."[6]

If the character trait of temperance involves moderation in all things, the prevalence of overeating among Christians—and especially among pastors—needs to be confronted. A 1997 survey of Southern Baptist pastors revealed that 60 percent of those surveyed (including their spouses) were overweight. More than 47 percent were, according to medical definition, obese. While only a small percentage of these pastors regularly ate breakfast, 61 percent nonetheless reported eating donuts and pastries. Forty-eight percent ate lunch in fast-food restaurants at least twice a week. Seventy-five percent reported eating fried foods for dinner at least four nights a week. And 40 percent admitted to snacking two or more times a day on cookies, chips, and candy.[7]

The truth is, such eating habits are common everywhere in America today. Why should we be concerned? As preachers, why should we choose to practice moderation in our eating even when few others choose to? The short answer is that God calls us to. As already seen, the life of an elder is to be marked by a pattern of temperance and moderation in all things (1 Tim. 3:2). For preachers, the practice of moderation in eating is especially important. Here's why.

First, habitual overeating reduces our longevity and effectiveness in ministry. Dr. Kenneth Cooper, fitness expert and founder of the Cooper Institute for Aerobics Research, was slapped hard by this truth when he was only twenty-nine years old. Cooper was a college athlete. However, during the years immediately following graduation, he adopted a sedentary lifestyle and added forty pounds to his frame. His blood pressure rose, and a day of even moderate work sapped his energy, leaving him exhausted. His wake-up call came when friends invited him to go waterskiing.

Although it had been ten years since he last skied, he decided to tackle the slalom course on his first run. He writes, "The extra forty pounds I was carrying, plus my greatly diminished muscle tone and endurance, were a formula for disaster." In fact, disaster almost happened. As he maneuvered through the course, Cooper quickly tired to a state of exhaustion, and his flabby body began to go numb. Somehow, he struggled back to the beach and collapsed. His heart raced dangerously. Fortunately, during the next thirty minutes, his heart rate returned to normal. Dr. Cooper, a believer, reflects:

> I realized that I had no one to blame but myself for my close brush with medical emergency. I also started to understand, perhaps for the first time, that my body was truly a "temple of God," but a temple I had allowed to fall into sad disrepair. It was clearly up to me to keep that temple in shape if I hoped to live a complete life and fulfill the plans God had for my life.[8]

The life-changing lesson Dr. Cooper learned is a lesson for all of us. While the food we eat is "created by God and to be received with thanksgiving"[9] (this is not a call to asceticism), like all good gifts it must be enjoyed responsibly. Irresponsible eating to the point of excessive weight gain can rob us of energy today and cost us years of useful service tomorrow. While those extra pounds may seem harmless at the moment, U.S. Surgeon General David Satcher recently stated, "Overweight and obesity may soon cause as much preventable disease and death as cigarette smoking."[10]

As preachers, it's time to step back and consider our eating habits. Do we eat and drink for the glory of God?[11] Are we exercising stewardship over our bodies in a way that enables us to proclaim the good news of Christ with all the energy and longevity God has ordained for us? Do we see what Dr. Cooper came to see—that my body is truly a "temple of God," and it is up to me to keep that temple in shape if I hope to live a complete life and fulfill the plans God has for my life?

But not only does God call preachers to be temperate for the sake of efficiency and longevity in his service. When it comes to eating, God calls us to be temperate for the sake of credibility. Like it or not, people do make judgments based on our appearance. This is especially true when it comes to first impressions. One author of a century ago reflects on this reality, writing, "The first impression of ourselves *and of our truth* is made through the physical life, and to have that impression pleasant and attractive cannot be beneath the attention of a Christian minister" (emphasis mine).[12]

Fair or not—and often it is fair—to many people obesity communicates a lack of discipline and self-control. For such people an overweight or obese preacher becomes an obstacle to hearing and accepting the life-changing truth of Christ. And even when we preach to those who know and love us, how can we effectively proclaim moderation if our appearance contradicts our words?

If we're serious about pleasing God and preaching his Word effectively and credibly, we ought to be serious about practicing temperance when we eat. Beyond credibility, there's another motivation for us to exercise temperance in regard to food—love. If we love the people we minister to like God loves them, our practice of moderation is essential. For the sake of our brothers and sisters in Christ, we need to control our weight.

During the past ten years, I can remember drinking only one glass of wine. Even though Scripture contains no absolute prohibition against moderate drinking, I am now determined not to drink even one glass in the future. Why? Out of concern for those I pastor. While moderate drinking is no sin, Romans 14 makes it clear that causing others to stumble is. In a world where alcohol destroys many lives and families, I want to be certain that no one uses me, their pastor, as an excuse to do what for them may be spiritually and physically destructive.

Today, it seems that this same principle should be applied to our eating habits. Between 1976 and 1980, 46 percent of American adults were medically classified as being overweight. Fourteen percent were classified as being obese. Today, 64.5 percent (127 million) of American adults are overweight and 30.5 percent (60 million) are obese. Nine million Americans are severely obese.[13]

The tragedy of this increasing prevalence of obesity in our nation cannot be dismissed. Today, in the United States, 300,000 deaths every year are associated with obesity and being overweight. Obesity increases a person's risk of developing diseases, including high blood pressure, type 2 diabetes, heart disease, stroke, gallbladder disease, and cancer of the breast, prostate, and colon.[14]

The destructive societal impact of weight gain and obesity has become so severe that one medical journal published an article calling on community leaders (including clergy) to lose weight as a matter of ethical principle. The author declares:

> Not only physicians should accept *the practical ethics and moral responsibility* of attaining an optimum BMI (body mass index). I also think that others in our community in positions of responsibility and from whom leadership is to be expected should also accept that their example is primary. Politicians, *clergy*, police and moral philosophers must lead the way in physical fitness if we are to expect to reap the benefits of a lean society (emphasis mine).[15]

With so many around us suffering the self-destructive impact of obesity, we as pastors have a biblical mandate to control our weight and model temperance in our use of food. In Romans 12:2, Paul exhorts us, "Do not conform any longer to the pattern of this world, but be transformed by the renewing of your mind." Perhaps it's time for us to admit that we, the body of Christ, have allowed ourselves to be conformed to the pattern of this world in the way we eat. Too many believers eat the wrong things, eat too much of it, and are literally dying because of it. It is doubtful that repentance can happen in the church if it doesn't first happen among her pastors. Freedom from bondage to food and physical sloth must begin with us. We must preach temperance. We must model it.

Where do we begin? We begin by seeking God's strength. On the surface the solution to obesity is simple. Eat less. Exercise more. However, we all know that moderating eating habits, exercising consistently, and losing weight are easier said than done. Proper diet and weight loss requires self-discipline and perseverance. We need strength, patience, and the daily grace of God.

We also need a plan.[16] In regard to exercise, Kenneth Cooper advises, "Don't start too fast. If you start too fast, there will be injuries and you will quit. Accept the fact that it will take a long time. You don't get out of shape rapidly, and it will take a while to get back in shape. Fitness is a journey, not a destination."[17]

On this journey most preachers find it difficult to set aside the time required to exercise regularly. The primary solution to this is to make exercise the priority it needs to be. We make time for things that are important to us. Another solution might be found in "doubling up" activities. For instance, the time that exercise requires can also be used for prayer or Scripture memory. Over a three-month period I was able to memorize the Sermon on the Mount during workouts on a treadmill. Having preached through the Sermon on the Mount "piece by piece," I was able to close the series by reciting it in its entirety. Not surprisingly, the congregation proclaimed it to be one of the best sermons I ever "preached."

For every preacher, modeling temperance is both essential and doable. Several years ago, a Doctor of Ministry class met for the first time. At the end of their two-week session, they exchanged prayer requests. One pastor asked his classmates to pray that he would be able to lose 100 pounds before they met together again. When the group gathered the following year, they recognized immediately that their prayers had been answered. Celebrating together, they asked their classmate how his victory had been achieved. He answered simply, "Every time I sat down for a meal, I bowed my head and prayed, "Holy Spirit, help me control my appetite." That's a prayer we can all pray. That's a prayer God will answer.

PART 3

HOW INTEGRITY GROWS

12

~~~~~~

PRACTICING SPIRITUAL DISCIPLINES

People we admit to be far greater than we are . . . found it necessary to practice disciplines and engage in activities with which we
blithely dispense. A John Wesley, a John Knox, a Martin Luther,
a George Fox, as well as a Paul may be admired in word. But in
reality we must think that they were a little fanatical or silly, for few
of us think enough of the practices they found necessary to adopt
them ourselves.

Dallas Willard, *The Spirit of the Disciplines*[1]

The titles are inviting. In the face of day planners bursting at the
seams and a world that demands nonstop activity, they even offer
hope. Hope that we might yet be able to squeeze God into our
schedules. Hope that a *One Minute Bible* can bring us into his presence.
Hope that *Seven Minutes with God* will be enough to deepen our walk
with him. These titles catch our attention because they promise (or
at least imply) a "quick fix" for our spiritual doldrums. We want to
reap spiritual growth by following three easy steps or by investing
ten minutes a day. In the struggle against our own depravity, we'd
rather say yes to a spiritual fad than say no to our sin nature. As

preachers, it's time to accept reality. Knowing God and growing up in Christ is hard work. The spiritual growth that is to mark our lives is a process—sometimes grueling, sometimes mundane—that requires the persistent practice of spiritual disciplines.

The word *disciplines* reminds us that human effort is required for spiritual growth. Paul teaches this in 1 Timothy 4:7 where he instructs, "Train yourself to be godly." Here Paul uses the Greek verb from which the English words *gymnastics* and *gymnasium* are derived. The term clearly relates to athletics. The picture Paul draws is of an athlete who subjects himself to a regimen of stringent discipline in pursuit of a goal. With this picture Paul suggests that a godly life cannot be realized apart from a believer's subjection to a similar regimen of strenuous discipline.

This, however, raises a question. Doesn't the suggestion that human effort makes a believer holy contradict the biblical truth that salvation is God's work from start to finish? Author Richard Foster answers that, rather than negating God's grace, the work of spiritual disciplines is actually a means of grace. He writes:

> The apostle Paul says, "he who sows to his flesh will from his flesh reap corruption; but he who sows to the Spirit will reap from the Spirit eternal life" (Galatians 6:8). Paul's analogy is instructive. A farmer is helpless to grow grain; all he can do is provide the right conditions for the growing of grain. He cultivates the ground, he plants the seed, he waters the plants, and then the natural forces of the earth take over and up comes the grain. This is the way it is with the Spiritual Disciplines—they are a way of sowing to the Spirit. The Disciplines are God's way of getting us into the ground; they put us where he can work with us and transform us. By themselves the Spiritual disciplines can do nothing; they can only get us to the place where something can be done. They are God's means of grace. The inner righteousness we seek is not something that is poured on our heads. God has ordained the Disciplines of the spiritual life as the means by which we place ourselves where he can bless us.
>
> In this regard it would be proper to speak of "the path of disciplined grace." It is "grace" because it is free; it is "disciplined" because there is something for us to do.[2]

In light of this, spiritual disciplines can never be seen as ends in themselves. This would be legalism. Foster's comments remind us that even as we exert the effort spiritual disciplines require, we must believe Jesus' admonition: "Apart from me you can do nothing." It is God's grace that makes spiritual disciplines effective. It is God's grace that changes our lives. Jonathan Edwards lived with this awareness. Edwards diligently pursued personal holiness through the practice of a series of spiritual disciplines he framed as seventy "resolutions." Remembering his ultimate dependence on grace, Edwards introduced his resolutions with a plea, "Being sensible that I am unable to do any thing without God's help, I do humbly entreat him, by his grace, to enable me to keep these Resolutions, so far as they are agreeable to his will, for Christ's sake."[3]

What, then, are the spiritual disciplines a pastor ought to practice by God's grace? Without doubt, prayer is critical to any preacher's ministry and to his growth in godliness. The example of Christ teaches this. At times Jesus chose solitude and prayer over face-to-face ministry to people in need. Luke 5:15–16 reports, "Yet the news about him spread all the more, so that crowds of people came to hear him and to be healed of their sicknesses. *But Jesus often withdrew to lonely places and prayed.*" In the same way Matthew 14:23; Mark 1:35; Luke 6:12; 9:18; 9:28; and 11:1 reveal Christ's commitment to private prayer. If Jesus Christ, God the Son, saw a need to regularly withdraw and pray, can we who preach his Word claim we have no such need?

That the apostles recognized their need to pray is demonstrated by the events of Acts 6:1–4. Luke writes:

> In those days when the number of disciples was increasing, the Grecian Jews among them complained against the Hebraic Jews because their widows were being overlooked in the daily distribution of food. So the Twelve gathered all the disciples together and said, "It would not be right for us to neglect the ministry of the word of God in order to wait on tables. Brothers, choose seven men from among you who are known to be full of the Spirit and wisdom. We will turn this responsibility over to them and *will give our attention to prayer* and the ministry of the word."

The apostles linked the ministry of the Word (preaching) to the ministry of prayer. For them prayer was a primary calling and they refused to be distracted from it.

In the same way, Paul's life exemplifies our need to commit ourselves to the discipline of prayer. An inspection of his epistles offers the clear evidence that Paul was, in fact, a man who "prayed without ceasing." To the Romans he writes, "God . . . is my witness how constantly I remember you in my prayers at all times."[4] In 1 Corinthians 1:4 he claims, "I always thank God for you." To the Ephesians he likewise states, "I have not stopped giving thanks for you, remembering you in my prayers."[5] He similarly refers to his faithful praying in Philippians 1:3–4; Colossians 1:3; 1 Thessalonians 1:2–3; 3:10; 2 Thessalonians 1:11; 2 Timothy 1:3; and Philemon 4–6. By his example Paul teaches that the call to preach can never be separated from the call to pray for those we preach to.

In light of these examples, few of us deny the importance of prayer to our spiritual growth and usefulness in ministry. Unfortunately, knowing the importance of prayer and actually making prayer a significant part of our lives are two different things. At least one survey suggests that many preachers are frustrated in their struggle to make time for prayer. This survey of 572 American pastors revealed that 57 percent pray less than 20 minutes a day; 34 percent pray between 20 minutes and an hour a day; 9 percent pray more than an hour a day. The survey also revealed that the average daily prayer time for pastors was 22 minutes a day while 28 percent (more than one in four) prayed less than ten minutes daily.[6]

When these statistics are read against the backdrop of the lives of men like Martin Luther, John Wesley, or E. M. Bounds, discouragement can easily set in. Luther reportedly proclaimed, "I have so much business, I can not get on without spending three hours daily in prayer." Wesley's prayer room has been called the "powerhouse of Methodism." And E. M. Bounds prayed from 4 a.m. until 7 a.m. each day. Here Foster's comments are especially helpful:

> Many of us . . . are discouraged rather than challenged by such examples. Those "giants of the faith" are so far beyond anything we have experienced that we are tempted to despair. But rather than

flagellating ourselves for our obvious lack, we should remember that God always meets us where we are and slowly moves us along into deeper things. Occasional joggers do not suddenly enter an Olympic marathon. They prepare and train themselves over a period of time, and so should we. When such a progression is followed, we can expect to pray a year from now with greater authority and spiritual success than at present.[7]

How do we begin to exercise this discipline of prayer more faithfully? First, we should honestly evaluate the present condition of our prayer lives. If we discover ourselves lacking, we can set a reasonable goal—maybe to pray 20 to 25 minutes a day (the reported average for pastors). Choose a specific time and place to pray. Write it into your schedule. Then show up. If we start by consistently praying for 20 to 25 minutes a day, we will grow and ultimately find ourselves praying longer and more effectively.

As pastors, another means of fostering growth in our prayer lives is to make a conscious effort to "practice the presence of God." We need to work at maintaining an ongoing conversation with our Lord throughout the day. Paul has this in mind when he exhorts us to "pray without ceasing" (1 Thess. 5:17 KJV).

None of these suggestions are new or earth shattering. Still, most of us need to be reminded of them regularly. Spurgeon's words are convicting, but they offer a needed challenge: "Of course the preacher is above all others distinguished as a man of prayer. He prays as an ordinary Christian, else he were a hypocrite. He prays more than ordinary Christians, else he were disqualified for the office he has undertaken."[8]

Closely associated with prayer is the spiritual discipline of fasting. Jesus speaks of this discipline, instructing:

When you fast, do not look somber as the hypocrites do, for they disfigure their faces to show men they are fasting. I tell you the truth, they have received their reward in full. But when you fast, put oil on your head and wash your face, so that it will not be obvious to men that you are fasting, but only to your Father who is unseen; and your Father, who sees what is done in secret will reward you.[9]

Here we discover that Jesus assumes that his followers will fast. In Matthew 5:16 Jesus says, "When you fast," not "If you fast." He says, "When you fast" just like he says, "When you give" (v. 2) and "When you pray" (v. 5). If Jesus intends giving and praying to be a normal part of the Christian life, he intends fasting to be as well.

But how should we fast? In this same passage Jesus tells us that, normally, we should fast secretly. By fasting secretly we avoid the temptation to use fasting as a means to impress our congregations with how spiritual we are. Fasting is of no value if our motives are wrong. Jesus says that in most cases the decision to fast ought to be a private one. Of course, there are times when churches or nations rightly choose to fast corporately. In these cases, fasting cannot be done in secret.

There are a number of biblical reasons to fast. Two are especially relevant to preachers. First, fasting is a means of expressing humility before God. One of the dangers of pastoring is the temptation to believe (or act like we believe) that the effectiveness of our ministries ultimately depends on us. Fasting is an act of humility before God. By fasting we acknowledge our dependence on him. This was the purpose of the fast Ezra speaks of in Ezra 8:21. The Israelites were embarking on a dangerous journey from Babylon to Jerusalem. How did they prepare for their journey? Ezra reports, "There by the Ahava Canal, I proclaimed a fast, *so that we might humble ourselves before our God* and ask him for a safe journey for us and our children."

Ezra recognized that the success of his ministry and Israel's journey depended on God. Fasting was the way he and the nation expressed that humble dependence. In the same way, fasting provides pastors with a means to actively humble themselves before God and acknowledge their dependence on him in their ministry of preaching.

The second reason for fasting is its capacity to express or deepen urgency in prayer. Most often, fasting in the Bible is associated with fervent prayer. Often, it is not clear which comes first—fasting or urgency in prayer. In some cases a sense of urgency may move one to fast. In others, it may be the act of fasting that deepens urgency. In either case the example of Moses offers a challenge to all who lead God's people and preach God's Word. In Deuteronomy

9:18–19, Moses describes how he pleaded with God and prayed for his congregation when they sinned by worshiping the golden calf. The depth of his burden is evident as he recounts:

> Once again I fell prostrate before the Lord for forty days and forty nights; *I ate no bread and drank no water, because of all the sin you had committed*, doing what was evil in the Lord's sight and so provoking him to anger. I feared the anger and the wrath of the Lord, for he was angry enough with you to destroy you. But again the Lord listened to me.

I wonder. As pastors, how often are we so burdened for our congregations that we willingly plead for them with *both* prayer and fasting? Fasting isn't magic. It doesn't guarantee that God will answer our prayers exactly the way we want them answered. Still, the urgency in prayer Moses expressed by fasting made all the difference for the people of his congregation. That same urgency, expressed in the same way, might make the difference for the people we love and preach to as well.

But prayer and fasting are not the only disciplines necessary for our spiritual growth as preachers. Time spent studying and reflecting on God's Word is essential to the maturing of any believer. Paul emphasizes the importance of Scripture for the preacher's growth in 2 Timothy 3:16–17 when he reminds his co-worker, "All Scripture is God-breathed and is useful for teaching, rebuking, correcting and training in righteousness, *so that the man of God may be thoroughly equipped for every good work.*"

While these words legitimately apply to all believers, in context they are specifically addressed to Timothy the preacher. He is "the man of God" being thoroughly equipped for every good work in ministry. Like Timothy, our ultimate usefulness as pastors rests, at least in part, on our willingness to allow God's Word to teach, rebuke, correct, and train us in righteousness. Only when we ourselves are being shaped by God's Word are we equipped to proclaim it to others.

Ezra's life and ministry exemplifies this principle. Ezra 7:10 reveals why God's "gracious hand" was on this great teacher of

Israel. We learn that "Ezra had devoted himself to the study and the observance of the Law of the LORD, and to teaching its decrees and laws in Israel." Before Ezra attempted to teach God's Word to others, he first disciplined himself to "study and observe" it himself. The righteous character that made him useful to God was rooted in his disciplined study of Scripture.

Of course, the Bible study Ezra engaged in was more than an intellectual pursuit. Knowing Bible facts is never enough. Meditating on Scripture, with an eye towards obeying it is what made Ezra such an effective instrument in God's hand. Foster reminds us:

> The discipline of meditation was certainly familiar to the authors of Scripture. The Bible uses two different Hebrew words to convey the idea of meditation, and together they are used some fifty-eight times. These words have various meanings: listening to God's word, reflecting on God's works, rehearsing God's deeds, ruminating on God's law, and more.[10]

The essence of biblical meditation is the act of reflecting on how a specific passage of Scripture is to be applied and obeyed in our own life and circumstances. How do the promises of Scripture apply to me in my struggles? Where does God's Word confront me concerning my attitudes? Only when we meditate on Scripture this way can it equip us by "teaching, rebuking, correcting, and training us in righteousness."

Prayer, fasting, and personal Bible study are just some of the spiritual disciplines God uses to produce righteousness in a preacher's life. As preachers, we must not let busyness squeeze these disciplines out of our lives. Speaking pastor to pastor, Eugene Peterson asks—and I believe correctly answers—a critical question:

> What are the actual means by which I carry out this pastoral vocation, this ordained ministry, the professional commitment to God's word and God's grace in my life and in the lives of the people to whom I preach? . . . The answer among the masters whom I consult doesn't change: a trained attentiveness to God in prayer, in Scripture reading, in spiritual direction. This has not been tried and discarded because it didn't work, but tried and

found difficult (and more than a little bit tedious) and so shelved in favor of something or other that could be fit into a busy pastor's schedule.[11]

As preachers, we ought to take care not to discard the grace God offers us through the practice of spiritual disciplines. By practicing these disciplines we grow in godliness. By growing in godliness our preaching grows in power.

13

THE PRACTICE
OF EXPOSITORY PREACHING

To preach is to deal with the raw materials of faith; so when I preach
great truths of Scripture, I am molded by them even as God uses the
same passages to shape others through me.

Neil Wiseman, *The Heart of a Great Pastor*[1]

They come via the mail or the Internet with regularity. One reads,
"Give your sermons a jump-start!" According to the ad, these
easy to use outlines may be just what I need to take my sermons from
good to great. Another mailing promises that I can, "Prepare exciting
sermons IN HALF THE TIME"! Prepare? If I say yes to this offer every
four to six weeks I'll receive "five carefully developed sermons, each
of which can be taken straight to the pulpit . . ." And, of course, there
is my all-time favorite, "Pastor Frank's Secret Weapon." It tells the
moving story of how Pastor Frank's ministry, marriage, and emotional
health were all saved by a library of Bible outlines available for only
$19.97 a month.

One of these advertisements asks the busy pastor this question
concerning sermon preparation, "Wouldn't it be wonderful if you

could eliminate most of the page-turning and looking up? What if a team of experts had already done most of the busywork for you"? No, as a matter of fact, it wouldn't be wonderful. And that "busy work"? It may be drudgery. But it's necessary drudgery. Necessary for the growth of the preacher. Necessary for the growth of the church.

The hard work of sermon preparation should not be avoided. Nor should its importance as a means of spiritual growth be overlooked by any pastor. In study, our goal should not simply be "to get a sermon." Whenever we prepare sermons, we ought to be pursuing deeper intimacy with Christ. Robert Murray M'Cheyne reminds us of this in his letter to a friend preparing for ordination:

> The grand matter of study, however, must still be divinity—a knowledge of divine things, a spiritual discernment of the way of pardon for the chief of sinners. I feel that the best of ministers are but babes in this . . . Pray for glorious discoveries of Christ—His person, beauty, work, and peace.[2]

Specifically, it is the practice of expository preaching that—more than other methods—lead us into such "glorious discoveries of Christ." Haddon Robinson defines expository preaching as

> the communication of a biblical concept, derived from and transmitted through a historical, grammatical, and literary study of a passage in its context, which the Holy Spirit first applies to the personality and experience of the preacher, then through the preacher, applies to the hearers.[3]

For preachers, expository preaching is a means of spiritual growth because it forces us to engage God's Word at a deep level. It is possible to prepare a topical sermon by first developing an outline and then skimming the surface of Scripture to find texts that support the outline's theme. A mere skimming of Scripture's surface, however, is not adequate for preparing expository sermons. By definition, expository preaching requires a pastor to dive into the deep end of one biblical text. However, taking this plunge in a way that leads to spiritual growth requires a teachable heart. Again Robinson writes:

Expository preaching at its core is more a philosophy than a method. Whether or not we can be called expositors starts with our purpose and with our honest answer to the question: "Do you as a preacher, endeavor to bend your thought to the Scriptures, or do you use the Scriptures to support your thoughts?" . . . In approaching a passage, we must be willing to reexamine our doctrinal convictions and to reject the judgments of our most respected teachers. We must make a U-turn in our own previous understandings of the Bible should these conflict with the concepts of the biblical writer.[4]

Armed with this willingness to take their beliefs wherever Scripture leads, expository preachers seek the objective meaning of their weekly sermon text by studying it in its "historical, grammatical, and literary" context. Concerning this process, Stott exhorts:

We shall need in particular to apply ourselves to the verse or passage selected for exposition from the pulpit. We shall need strength of mind to eschew short cuts. We must spend time studying our text with painstaking thoroughness, meditating on it, wrestling with it, worrying at it as a dog with a bone, until it yields its meaning; and sometimes this process will be accompanied by toil and tears.[5]

Through this process of "meditating on and wrestling with" a biblical text we are mentally stretched. The pastor who studies deeply will begin to think deeply. Mistaken beliefs are challenged. Wrong attitudes are surfaced in our minds. And this is where the process must not stop. Growth in godliness requires more than thinking deeply about God's Word. Growth requires the application of truth. Expository preaching's potency to transform the preacher is found in its insistence that truth be applied to self before it is preached to others. Again, Robinson's definition states that expository preaching is "the communication of a biblical concept . . . *which the Holy Spirit first applies to the personality and experience of the preacher*, then through the preacher, applies to the hearers" (emphasis mine).

Real expository preaching requires the application of a biblical truth to life. The starting point for this application must be the preacher himself. Robinson continues:

A commitment to expository preaching should develop the preacher into a mature Christian. As we study our Bible, the Holy Spirit studies us. As we prepare expository sermons, God prepares us. As P. T. Forsyth said, "The Bible is the supreme preacher to the preacher."

. . . Before we proclaim the message of the Bible to others, we should live with that message ourselves.[6]

In sermon preparation, learning to live with God's message is where growth happens in a preacher's life. How easy it is for us to shine Scripture's light on the congregation without first shining it on ourselves. Yielding to this temptation strips a sermon of power and a preacher of integrity. Bridges warns, "The best of us probably are far more spiritual in our pulpits than in our closets, and find less effort required to preach against all the sins of our people, than to mortify one of them in our own hearts."[7] In another place he adds, "We must ourselves taste the word, before we distribute it to our people. We must carefully connect it with our devotional reading. A sermon, however well digested, can never be well preached, until it has been first preached to ourselves."[8]

Preparing an expository sermon, then, must never become a mere intellectual exercise. By definition it is a spiritual exercise that involves both our hearts and our minds. Expository preaching is the discovery of a biblical truth found in one specific text of Scripture applied first to our own lives, and only then, to the lives of those in the congregation. Rightly practiced, expository preaching drives the pastor deep into God's Word, and God's Word deep into the pastor's heart. Thus, a preacher's place is a place of privilege. In the labor of weekly sermon preparation, we enjoy an opportunity for spiritual growth available to few others. Each week our opportunity is fully realized when, digging deeply, we let God's Word speak to us even as we prepare to speak God's Word to others.

"Jump-starts for sermons"? "Exciting sermons IN HALF THE TIME"? "Pastor Frank's Secret Weapon"? Such ads might offer easy sermons for $19.97 a month, but they do not offer food for our souls. Watch out for hidden costs.

14

<hr>

GROWING BY STAYING

Honorable men will not toy with churches. There is something
of the sacredness of marriage in the pastoral relation and when
once entered on it is for better or for worse. Short pastorates are
unfortunate both for pastors and people.

Charles Jefferson, *Quiet Hints to Growing Preachers in My Study*[1]

He sat across the table explaining why he was leaving his church
after only a brief ministry. "The people in my church," he said,
"are too busy with their own lives. They're too laid back. They're
not committed to giving God their best. Sometimes I think they
care more about their houses than about Christ." As I listened, I
wondered if this pastor had considered the possibility that God had
brought him to his church so he might stay and, over the course
of time, lead the congregation from where they presently were to
where they needed to be.

It is no secret that many American pastors change churches
often. *Your Church* reports, "In a 1997 survey of pastors, George
Barna found that the average pastor stayed at a church for five years.
Other surveys list an even more frequent turnaround."[2]

It must be stated up front that some blame for this lack of pastoral longevity lies with churches themselves. Unresponsive, contentious, or stingy congregations make it easy—and sometimes necessary—for pastors to leave. Still, even when this is accounted for, it seems certain that many pastors suffer from a destructive kind of wanderlust. Somehow we have lost sight of the fact that preachers who continually drift from congregation to congregation stifle not just the church's growth, but also their own.

The harmful impact of short pastorates was well understood in past generations. During the Reformation, Calvin knew that valid reasons existed for pastors to change churches. Even so he counseled:

> But he who is called to one place ought not to think of leaving or to seek release (considering it to be to his advantage). Then, if it be expedient for anyone to be transferred to another place, still he ought not to attempt this on his own private resolve, but to await public authority.[3]

Later, nineteenth-century Scottish pastor Andrew Bonar likewise wrote:

> Few godly pastors can be willing to change the scene of their labors, unless it be plain that the Cloudy Pillar is pointing them away. It is perilous for men to choose for themselves; and too often has it happened that the minister who, on slight grounds, moved away from his former watch-tower, has had reason to mourn over the disappointment of his hopes in his larger and wider sphere.[4]

It was by their practice that Puritan ministers demonstrated their belief that the call to preach is most often a call to minister long-term with one congregation. Theologian David Wells writes:

> It was typical in the eighteenth century for a church and its minister to enter into a compact that was sometimes legal in character but always morally binding and generally understood to last for the duration of the minister's life. It was possible for a minister to move from one church to another, but only with the consent

of both the original church and the surrounding churches (in the case of the Congregationalists) or those in the presbytery (in the case of the Presbyterians).[5]

Between 1745 and 1775, 221 students graduated from Yale and entered the ministry. Wells notes that 71 percent of these men remained in the church that first called them until their deaths. Only 4 percent held four or more pastorates during their lives.[6] When considering these statistics we should not forget that Puritan America was a far less mobile society than ours. Even so, the fact that seven out of ten pastors served one church for life speaks of their belief that long-term ministry in one place is God's norm for preachers.

Ultimately, of course, the cautions of a Reformer and the practice of Puritans do not decisively prove that long pastorates are preferable to short ones. What does Scripture say? No specific Bible passage directly commands pastors to minister long-term in one church. Nonetheless, two biblical principles support the premise that ministering long-term with one congregation is God's intent for most of us. First, the Bible teaches that every pastor is accountable for those ministered to.

In Hebrews 13:17, believers are instructed, "Obey your leaders and submit to their authority. They keep watch over you *as men who must give an account.*" If we are accountable for the spiritual well-being of those we shepherd, we must put their eternal welfare above our personal desires and "career" goals. Whenever we consider a move we must consider the impact our departure will have on our present congregation. We must ask if our departure will ultimately benefit our present flock or damage them. This does not mean we can *never* leave one church for another. It does mean that, if we are wise, we will not be quick to do so. Because of accountability, much prayer and an honest examination of our motives are prerequisites to leaving one church for another. As preachers we must always remember that we will be held responsible for any damage we cause a congregation because of an ill-advised or selfish move.

A second biblical principle that challenges a "have Bible—will travel" mentality is that of imitation. As pastors, we are Christ's under-shepherds (1 Peter 5:2–4). In our ministries we must imitate Jesus, the Chief Shepherd. We learn what this means in John 10:11–13 where Jesus explains:

> I am the good shepherd. The good shepherd lays down his life for the sheep. The hired hand is not the shepherd who owns the sheep. So when he sees the wolf coming, he abandons the sheep and runs away. Then the wolf attacks the flock and scatters it. The man runs away because he is a hired hand and cares nothing for the sheep.

If we, as pastors, are Christ's under-shepherds, then, like Christ, we are called to lay down our lives—our personal dreams, our ambitions, and our goals—for the sheep (the people of our congregations). It is the hired hand who runs away (to the next church?) because his heart is never really with the sheep at all. Can a pastor who loves the flock like Jesus loves them easily leave? Does the pastor who habitually leaves one flock after another demonstrate Christ's love for them at all? Certainly, many pastors may be led by God's Spirit to serve more than one church during a lifetime of ministry. Still, pastors who never pledge themselves long-term to any congregation will likely fall short of fulfilling their call to model the love and faithfulness of Christ. The drawbacks of such "hired hand" pastoring were described by one writer a century ago:

> If a man knows he has but a short time in a parish he is tempted to do the things which are easiest and cheapest. He will not enter deeply into the hearts of his people but will be in danger of looking upon all laymen as so many pawns to be manipulated in an interesting game of ecclesiastical chess.[7]

By way of contrast, this same writer goes on to say:

> It is the long pastorate which draws on the fountains which are deepest and which builds up in congregation and pastor those elements of character in which the New Testament exults and rejoices. A man who expects to live with the same people through many years will have every incentive to be sane and industrious, far-sighted and true.[8]

Why, then, do relatively few pastors stay at one church for significant periods of time? The answer may lie in a mentality of professionalism commonly found among ministers today. Professionalism in ministry often leads preachers to approach the pastorate as a career rather than a calling. Wells writes:

> For if it is the case that careers can be had in the Church, then it is inevitable that ministers will be judged by the height to which they ascend on the ladder of achievement, and they in turn will judge the Church on the extent to which it facilitates this ascent. It is a little difficult to see how such calculations can be reconciled with the biblical notion of service, the call to serve the Church without thought of what one might receive in return.[9]

Eugene Peterson adds:

> Somehow we American pastors, without really noticing what was happening, got our vocations redefined in the terms of American careerism. We quit thinking of the parish as a location for pastoral spirituality and started thinking of it as an opportunity for advancement.[10]

The outcome of this "professional ministry" mind-set is that pastors often begin using their churches as rungs on a career ladder. No pastor can use a congregation this way and at the same time love them. Similarly, pastors motivated by their own career advancement will never consider the possibility that God might be calling them to pour their lives into the building up of one local church body.

But what about the small church? Doesn't a long-term commitment to serve a small church rob the gifted preacher of opportunities for a more "significant" ministry? If significance means leading a big congregation with multiple staff and a large budget, the answer is most definitely yes! Long-term commitment to one congregation will sometimes mean by-passing opportunities to serve a larger church. However, we must take care in how we define "significance." First, it is infinitely significant simply to be a child of God through faith in Christ. It is significant to be chosen by

God and adopted by him to be an heir of his unfathomable riches! Beyond this, how much more significant to be called to preach! The privilege of this "significance" is real whether we preach to a congregation of 25 or 2,500. Ultimately, the size of a pastor's congregation is no measure of significance in God's eyes. Most often, the significance of a preacher's ministry cannot be measured until generations have passed.

If we judged the ministries of Isaiah or Jeremiah based only on the visible impact they had on their contemporaries, both would be considered failures. With the passing of centuries, however, no one denies the eternal significance of their lives. Likewise, in his letters to the seven churches (Revelation 2–3), Jesus never commends any congregation based on its Sunday morning attendance. Instead, Smyrna and Philadelphia are singled out because of their faithfulness to the truth in the face of persecution. To the casual observer of that day, it is almost certain that these churches appeared to be insignificant. Even so, Jesus' praise of them still rings clear today.

And what of Jesus himself? If numbers are the ultimate measure of the significance of a ministry, Jesus didn't seem to know it. In John 6, Jesus drives away most of his disciples with his graphic and offensive preaching. At the time of his death and resurrection, Acts 1:15 reports that Jesus' Jerusalem congregation numbered only 120. Today we know that the significance of Christ's evangelistic ministry was never intended to be measured by that number. Rather, it must be measured by what God did in and through those 120 disciples after Jesus' departure.

In the same way, over a century ago, a Primitive Methodist lay preacher may have felt that his ministry was insignificant. On the Sunday morning he preached to just over a dozen people, it certainly looked insignificant. But it was on that morning Charles Spurgeon sat among those few and found new life in Christ. Is the man God used to reach Spurgeon less significant in heaven than Spurgeon himself? Likewise, under the ministry of a faithful pastor, one child in a small church (or perhaps that child's child) may grow up and touch thousands for Christ or, as a missionary, take the gospel to an unreached people group. Like a rock thrown into still waters, the influence of every preacher's ministry ripples across generations. This is why significance cannot be measured with the eye. This is why significance cannot be determined by the size of our congregations. God alone is the judge of significance. And his judgments will not be fully revealed this side of eternity.

It is tragic when a fear of insignificance drives a pastor away from God's chosen place of ministry. It is tragic when we cheat ourselves out of the benefits of serving one congregation over the long haul. What are those benefits? The answer is growth—growth in our effectiveness as preachers, growth in our spiritual lives.

Haddon Robinson reminds us that longevity generally increases our credibility, and thus, our effectiveness as preachers. He observes:

> Obviously one advantage of a lengthy ministry is that the pastor has a better chance to bring perception and reality together. The long-term pastor is judged more on his pattern of behavior than on a specific appearance. People are more likely to say, "The pastor not only talks love; he gives love. He was there in our family crisis when we needed him." A pattern of care can cover a multitude of less-than-stellar sermons.[11]

That long-term ministry increases our credibility as preachers is supported by a survey conducted by *Leadership*. Almost half of the survey's respondents (48 percent) ascribed authority to the sermons of pastors they had heard for more than fifteen years. For preachers heard for shorter periods of time, only 29 percent of the respondents ascribed authority to the sermons they heard.[12]

But not only can longevity enhance the effectiveness of our preaching, it can be a source of our own spiritual growth. Reflecting on the advantages of staying with one congregation, Eugene Peterson writes:

> The congregation is the pastor's place for developing vocational holiness.
>   It goes without saying that it is the place of ministry: we preach the word and administer the community life, we teach and we give spiritual direction. But it is also the place in which we develop

virtue, learn to love, advance in hope—*become* what we preach. At the same time we proclaim a holy gospel, we develop a holy life.[13]

A church is a family. At times, every family struggles through conflict and trials. Gossip destroys relationships. Sometimes pastors are confronted with unfair expectations. Disagreements arise over compensation or the direction ministry should take. Issues of church discipline divide the congregation. Some struggles are, for pastors, so intense and painful they are tempted to leave both the church and its problems behind. Responding this way can hinder God's purpose for our lives. James 1:2–4 exhorts:

> Consider it pure joy, my brothers, whenever you face trials of many kinds, because you know that the testing of your faith develops perseverance. Perseverance must finish its work so that you may be mature and complete, not lacking in anything.

It's easy to preach perseverance. It's far more difficult to practice it when things go sour in our churches. Persevering, however, is well worth the effort. James tells us that the fruit of persevering through trials (including those that pastors endure in their churches) is spiritual maturity. This means when we continually respond to church strife by running to a new church, we ultimately run away from our own potential growth. Likewise, by running from rather than confronting the congregation and its sin, we rob the church of an opportunity to repent, grow, and mature. This is why one writer advises, "Be not hasty to take up arms against a sea of troubles and attempt to end them by running away."[14]

Of course it is not simply facing struggles and trials that produces spiritual growth in the life of a pastor. Only a right response to trials brings maturity. When trials spring from wrongs committed against a pastor, the response God requires is forgiveness. In Colossians 3:13, Paul addresses a local church and commands, "Bear with each other and forgive whatever grievances you may have against one another. Forgive as the Lord forgave you." As pastors, we are a part of Christ's body. We are not exempt from this command. When wronged, "bearing with" our churches cannot mean stomping away to another church and taking our unresolved grudges with us. By staying and persevering we are forced to grow by learning God's way of forgiveness. Admittedly, this is not an easy lesson. When wounds cut deep forgiveness is hard. In the end, however, the course of unresolved bitterness is a harder course to run.

There are reasons to leave a church. At times God clearly calls us to new places of ministry. And some congregations really do make it impossible to stay. Still, pastors who stay long-term with one congregation have the opportunity not only to demonstrate integrity, but also to grow in it. We grow when we persevere through trials with our congregations. We grow when we learn to forgive others even as Christ has forgiven us.

As preachers we need to examine our hearts. We must ask ourselves—and answer honestly—"Do I view ministry as a career or a calling? Is the spiritual good of those I *presently* serve a priority when considering a move to another church? Am I a hired hand who runs at the first sign of trouble? Or am I a shepherd fully committed to the flock God assigns me?"

CONCLUSION

The call to preach is a call to live a life of integrity. In this life, we will never be perfect. Still our lives must be marked by spiritual maturity and continuing progress in the faith. The means of spiritual growth available to us for the strengthening of our character include the exercise of spiritual disciplines, the practice of expository preaching, and a commitment to minister long-term in a place of God's choosing. When we remember the nature and privilege of our calling we will strive to be faithful in that calling. In doing so, we will preach not only with our lips, but also with our lives. We will have integrity. Bridges reminds us, "The minister is a continual—not a periodical character . . . A holy sermon is but for an hour. A holy life is his perpetual sermon—a living practical commentary of his doctrine—the gospel to the senses."[1]

When all is said and done, the most powerful sermon your congregation hears is probably the one they see.

APPENDIX

VOICES FROM THE PAST

The call for integrity in a preacher's life has been heard throughout the course of church history. What follows are the words of faithful men who now surround us as a part of heaven's "great cloud of witnesses" (Heb. 12:1). May their words strengthen our resolve to "practice what we preach."

The First Epistle of Clement is believed to have been written in AD 95 or 96. In the epistle's thirteenth chapter entitled, "What Priests Should Be and Should Not Be," the author addresses the necessity of a minister's integrity, pleading:

> Let us, therefore, "ask of the Lord of the harvest" that He would send forth workmen into the harvest; such workmen as "shall skillfully dispense the word of truth;" workmen "who shall not be ashamed;" faithful workmen; workmen who shall be "the light of the world;" . . . not workmen who imitate the children of light, while they are not light but darkness—"men whose end is destruction;" not workmen who practice iniquity and wickedness and fraud; not "crafty workmen;" not workmen "drunken and faithless;" nor workmen who traffic in Christ; not misleaders; not "lovers of money; not malevolent."

Let us, therefore, contemplate and imitate the faithful who have
conducted themselves well in the Lord, as is becoming and suitable
to our calling and profession. Thus let us do service before God in
justice and righteousness, and without blemish, "occupying ourselves
with things good and comely before God *and* also before men."[1]

The belief that a minister's character is crucial to his effectiveness was also affirmed during the middle of the third century when
Christians suffered widespread persecution under Roman emperor
Decius. Under the pressure of this persecution many believers denied
their faith. Included among those who had "lapsed" were members
of the clergy. The Novatian Schism arose over the debate concerning
whether or not lapsed believers should be restored to the church.
An important element of that debate was whether lapsed clergy-
men could be restored to office. Peter, archbishop of Alexandria,
argued that such men should not be restored because, even though
their doctrine might be pure, they had failed to lead their flocks by
example. He argued:

> Whence it is not right either that those of the clergy who have deserted
> of their own accord, and have lapsed, and taken up the contest afresh
> should remain any longer in their sacred office, inasmuch as they have
> left destitute the flock of the Lord, and brought blame upon them-
> selves, which thing did not one of the apostles . . . who also would have
> him that teaches to be "in doctrine" an example to the faithful . . .
> But when they lapsed, as having carried themselves with ostentation,
> and brought reproach upon themselves, they can no longer discharge
> their sacred ministry; and, therefore, let them the rather take heed
> to pass their life in humility, ceasing from vainglory.[2]

In his commentaries, St. Chrysostom (347–407) anchors his
argument that the teacher of God's Word must live a holy life to two
truths. The first is that a teacher must not simply speak the truth
but also model it. In his homily on 1 Timothy, Chrysostom exhorts,
"In all things showing thyself an example of good works: that is, be
thyself a pattern of a Christian life, as a model set before others, as
a living law, as a rule and standard of good living, for such ought a
teacher to be."[3]

Likewise, in his homily on Titus he addressed those who would teach:

> And let the luster of thy life be a common school of instruction, a pattern of virtue to all, publicly exhibited like some original model, containing in itself all beauties affording examples whence those who are willing may easily imprint upon themselves any of its excellencies . . . For when the life is illustrious, and the discourse corresponds to it, being meek and gentle, and affording no handle to the adversaries, it is of unspeakable advantage.[4]

But the need to model the Christian truth we preach is not the only grounds from which Chrysostom argues for the priority of a preacher's integrity. The fear of judgment is also offered as motivation for preachers and teachers to keep their lives pure. Commenting on Matthew 23:3 Chrysostom wrote, "For what can be more wretched than a teacher, when the preservation of his disciples is, not to give heed to his life"?[5] Later in the same passage he continued:

> For every one is worthy of blame in transgressing the law, but especially he that bears the authority of teaching, for doubly and triply doth he deserve to be condemned. For one cause, because he transgresses; for another, that as he ought to amend others, and then halteth, he is worthy of a double punishment, because of his dignity; and in the third place, that he even corrupts the more, as committing such transgression in a teacher's place.[6]

The importance of a preacher's character was also recognized during the Reformation. While Luther writes little on the subject directly, he does deal with the issue in his commentary on Titus. In the following passage we see that, for Luther, a preacher's integrity has much to do with an honest handling and presentation of the biblical text. Luther wrote:

> You who are placed in their midst should be a pure pattern. A bishop ought to be held up to public view. If anything is desirable in others, it ought to be found in him. In what respect? . . . The chief thing in a bishop is that he set forth the Word correctly, because teaching is

his principal work, and he is to be devoted above all to the conservation of doctrine. Show, that is, in your doctrine show integrity, gravity, sound speech, and irreproachability. All four of these should be shown in his teaching: integrity, gravity, sound speech and irreproachability . . . In teaching, you will preserve and demonstrate integrity and incorruptibility, so that you do not adulterate the Word in teaching but teach a doctrine that is not mixed or diluted. This should be evident not only in your word, but in yourself, that you may be a sound teacher, one who is not at fault, one who does not vitiate the doctrine with his own opinions but presents the Word in its integrity as it has been entrusted to him.[7]

While Luther focuses on the necessity for a preacher to honestly proclaim God's Word, Calvin enlarged his field of vision and addressed the need for holiness in all areas of a minister's life. Concerning the election of elders, Calvin wrote:

In two passages [Titus 1:7; 1 Tim. 3:1–7] Paul fully sets forth what sort of bishops (i.e., elders) ought to be chosen. To sum up, only those are to be chosen who are of sound doctrine and of holy life, not notorious in any fault which might both deprive them of authority and disgrace the ministry [1 Tim. 3:2–3; Titus 1:7–8].[8]

In his commentary on the Pastoral Epistles he further states, "For doctrine will otherwise carry little authority if its power and majesty do not shine in the life of the bishop, as in a mirror."[9]

From the seventeenth through the nineteenth century the importance of the integrity of a preacher's life was emphasized by many writers. In *The Marrow of Theology*, first published in 1629, William Ames wrote:

Since first an earnest zeal for the church's edification is required, a man cannot be a fit preacher unless he has "Set his heart to study the law of the Lord and do it, and to teach his statutes and ordinances in Israel (Ezra 7:10)." For one who teaches another ought before and while he teaches to teach himself (Romans 2:21). Otherwise he is not prepared to edify the church.[10]

Puritan pastor Richard Baxter insists on the necessity of congruence between the life of the preacher and what he preaches. He exhorted:

Take heed to yourselves, lest you exemplify contradictory doctrine. Beware, lest you lay such stumbling blocks before the blind that you occasion their ruin. Beware, lest you undo with your lives, what you say with your tongues. Beware, lest you become the greatest hindrance to the success of your own labors. It hinders our work greatly when other men contradict in private what we have declared to them publicly about the Word of God. This is so because we cannot be there to contradict them and to show their folly.

But it will much more hinder our work if we contradict ourselves. If our actions become a lie to our tongues, then what we may build up in an hour or two of discourse can be demolished with our hands in a week. This is the way to make men think that the Word of God is merely an idle tale and to make preaching appear no better than prating. For he that means as he speaks will surely do as he speaks.[11]

Based on this reasoning, Baxter goes on to challenge all who would be preachers, "We must think, and think again, how to compose our lives (as well as our sermons) as may best lead to men's salvation."[12]

In Germany, Lutheran pastor Philip Jacob Spener published *Pia Desideria* in 1675. Like his Puritan counterparts he argued for the necessity of preachers to live God's Word as well as speak it. In order of importance—with regard to effectiveness in ministry—Spener chose godly character over academic achievement. He wrote:

Surely, students of theology ought to lay this foundation, that during their early years of study they realize that they must die unto the world and live as individuals who are to become examples to the flock, and that this is not merely an ornament but a very necessary work . . . It is certain that a young man who fervently loves God, although adorned with limited gifts, will be more useful to the church of God with his meager talent and academic achievement that a vain and worldly fool with double doctor's degrees who is very clever but has not been taught by God. The work of the former is blessed, and he is aided by the Holy Spirit. The latter has only a carnal knowledge, with which he can easily do more harm than good.[13]

Considered by many to be the greatest theologian America has ever produced, Jonathan Edwards also recognized the biblical demand for consistency between the preacher's life and message. In an ordination sermon preached August 30, 1744, Edwards instructed:

> God sent His Son into the world to be the light of the world in two ways, viz. By revealing his mind and will to the world, and also by setting the world a perfect example. So ministers are set to be lights, not only as teachers but as examples to the flock, I Peter 5:3.
>
> The same things that ministers recommend to their hearers in doctrine, they should also show them an example in their practice.[14]

John Wesley likewise makes the connection between the behavior of the messenger and the impact of the message in a letter of rebuke to a Methodist minister. He wrote, "Your temper is uneven; you lack love for your neighbors. You grow angry too easily; your tongue is too sharp—thus the people will not hear you."[15]

In the nineteenth century, the importance of the preacher's personal character was regularly emphasized by Bible-believing preachers and theologians. French preacher and teacher of homiletics Alexandre Vinet wrote:

> Preaching is an action, but an action of the soul, and its effects are connected with the preacher's spiritual state. It is not so much by what he says as by what he is that the preacher may flatter himself that he does not beat the air. Before every thing, he is concerned to "hold the mystery of the faith in a pure conscience" (I Timothy 3:9). This pure conscience (that is to say, uprightness of intention) is the true force of preaching.[16]

In his book *The Christian Ministry*, Charles Bridges lists the absence of godly character as a main cause for "ministerial inefficiency." Concerning the relationship between a minister's character and his success in preaching, Bridges wrote:

> We observe again the importance of personal religion in confirming our testimony with Christian example. Men judge things more

fully by the eye than by the ear; consequently Ministers' practice is as much regarded, if not more than their sermons.[17]

Continuing on the same theme he wrote,

They [the hearers] believe his life more than his talk, and when they know him to be selfish, ambitious, vain, given to sloth and luxury, and see that he parts with none of those enjoyments, which he exhorts others to forsake; though for the sake of custom and ceremony they hear him declaim, they believe and act as he does . . . We must build up with both hands—with our doctrine and our life. We must be what we preach . . . A holy sermon is but for an hour. A holy life is his perpetual sermon—a living, practical commentary of his doctrine—the gospel to the senses.[18]

Even more to the point is Bridges's statement, "A man who cannot persuade himself to be holy, will have little hope of succeeding with the consciences of others."[19]

The words of Robert Murray M'Cheyne closely align with those of Bridges. In an ordination sermon preached in 1840, M'Cheyne declared:

But oh, study universal holiness of life! Your whole usefulness depends on this. Your sermon on Sabbath lasts but an hour or two—your life preaches all week. Remember, ministers are standard-bearers. Satan aims his fiery darts at them. If he can only make you a covetous minister, or a lover of pleasure, or a lover of praise, or a lover of good eating, then he has ruined your ministry for ever.[20]

In a letter to a friend about to be ordained, M'Cheyne picked up the same theme:

Remember you are God's sword—His instrument—I trust a chosen vessel unto Him to bear His name. In great measure, according to the purity and perfections of the instrument, will be the success. It is not great talents God blesses so much as great likeness to Jesus. A holy minister is an awful weapon in the hand of God.[21]

In his 1872 Yale Lectures on Preaching, Henry Ward Beecher exhorted students concerning the requirement for moral integrity with these words:

> A part of your preparation for the Christian ministry consists in such a ripening of your disposition that you yourselves shall be exemplars of what you preach . . . You must come up to a much higher level than common manhood, if you mean to be a preacher.[22]

Explaining the practical necessity of the preacher's integrity Beecher went on to say:

> The first thing you have to do is to present to them what you want them to be. That is, if you are to preach to them faith, the best definition you can give of faith is to exercise it . . . If you would explain what true benevolence is, be yourselves before them that which you want them to understand and imitate.[23]

Five years after Beecher initiated the Yale Lectures on Preaching, Phillips Brooks ascended the same platform to deliver his famous lecture series. He too addressed the critical role the moral character of the preacher plays in the communication of God's Word. He stated, "And the first among the elements of power which make success I must put the supreme importance of character, of personal uprightness and purity impressing themselves upon the men who witness them."[24] Pointing to the shortest road to credibility, Brooks continued:

> Whatever strange and scandalous eccentricities the ministry has sometimes witnessed, this is certainly true, and is always encouraging, that no man permanently succeeds in it who cannot make men believe that he is pure and devoted, and the only sure and lasting way to make men believe in one's devotion and purity is to be what one wishes to be believed to be.[25]

No preacher of the nineteenth century spoke more clearly concerning the obligation of preachers to be men of integrity than did Charles Haddon Spurgeon. In *Lectures to My Students*, Spurgeon proclaimed, "Better abolish pulpits than fill them with men who have no experiential knowledge of what they teach."[26] It is not surprising, then, that Spurgeon believed that a genuine call to ministry is not a call that stands alone. He stated, "Whatever call a man may pretend to have, if he has not been called to holiness, he certainly has not been called to the ministry."[27]

E. M. Bounds also adamantly contended that, in preaching, the message and the messenger can never be separated. In his book *Power through Prayer*, he stated:

> We are continually striving to create new methods, plans, and organizations to advance the Church. We are ever working to provide and stimulate growth and efficiency for the gospel. This trend of the day has a tendency to lose sight of the man . . . God's plan is to make much of the man, far more of him than of anything else. Men are God's methods. The Church is looking for better methods; God is looking for better men.[28]

In another place Bounds added:

> Volumes have been written stating the detailed mechanics of sermon making. We have become possessed with the idea that this scaffolding is the building. The young preacher has been taught to exhaust all of his strength on the form, taste, and beauty of his sermon as a mechanical and intellectual product . . . We have emphasized eloquence instead of piety, rhetoric instead of revelation, reputation and brilliancy instead of holiness. By it, we have lost the true idea of preaching. We have lost preaching power, and the pungent conviction of sin.[29]

So as not to be misunderstood, Bounds went on to say, "We are not saying that men are not to think and use their intellects. But, he who cultivates his heart the most will use his intellect the best."[30] For Bounds, the primary means by which a preacher must cultivate his heart is prayer. Prayer is what empowers preaching. He wrote, "Talking to men for God is a great thing, but talking to God for men is still greater. He who has not learned well how to talk to God for men will never talk well—with real success—to men for God."[31]

Bounds added, "The preachers who gain mighty results for God are men who have prevailed in their pleadings with God *before* venturing to plead with men. The preachers who are mightiest in their closets with God are the mightiest in their pulpits with men."[32]

Perhaps Bounds best summed up the importance of a preacher's integrity when he wrote:

> The character as well as the fortunes of the gospel are committed to the preacher. He either makes or mars the message from God to man. The preacher is the golden pipe through which the divine oil flows. The pipe must not only be golden, but open and flawless. This way the oil may have a full, unhindered, and unwasted flow.
>
> The man makes the preacher. God must make the man. The messenger is, if possible, more than the message. The preacher is more than the sermon. The preacher *makes* the sermon. As life-giving milk from the mother's bosom is no more than the mother's life, so all the preacher says is tinctured, impregnated, by what the preacher *is*. The treasure is in earthen vessels, and the taste of the vessel may permeate and discolor the treasure. The man—the whole man lies behind the sermon. Preaching is not the performance of an hour. It is the outflow of a life. It takes twenty years to make a sermon, because it takes twenty years to make the man. The true sermon is a thing of life. The sermon grows because the man grows. The sermon is forceful because the man is forceful. The sermon is holy because the man is holy. The sermon is full of divine anointing because the man is full of divine anointing.[33]

May God by his grace cause his truth to flow unhindered and unwasted through us.

Notes

Introduction

1. *Epigraph*. C. H. Spurgeon, *Lectures to My Students* (Grand Rapids: Zondervan, 1954), 216.

2. Aristotle, *Rhetoric and Poetics of Aristotle*, trans. W. Rhys Roberts (New York: The Modern Library, 1954), 25.

3. *New Oxford American Dictionary* (New York: Oxford University Press, 2002).

Chapter 1 Integrity's Power to Persuade

1. *Epigraph*. John Wesley, *The Works of John Wesley*, vol. 7 (New York: 1831), 229; quoted in James L. Golden, Berquist R. Goodwin, and William E. Coleman, *The Rhetoric of Western Thought* (Dubuque, IA: Kendall/Hunt Publishing Co., 1983), 297.

2. John Selby Watson, *Quintilian's Institutes of Oratory*, vol. 2 (London: George Bell and Sons, 1876), 392.

3. Ibid., 394.

4. Robert K. Merton, *Mass Persuasion: The Social Psychology of a War Bond Drive* (New York: Harper and Brothers Publishers, 1946), 2–3.

5. Ibid., 84.

6. Ibid., 90.

7. Ibid., 93.

8. Ibid., 94.

9. Ibid.

10. Phillips Brooks, *Lectures on Preaching* (London: H. R. Allenson, Ltd., 1877), 51.

Chapter 2 Revisiting God's Call

1. *Epigraph*. D. Martyn Lloyd-Jones, *Preaching and Preachers* (Grand Rapids: Zondervan, 1977), 110.

2. John 15:13.

3. John 11:25.

4. Matthew 28:19.

5. John 4:1–42; Matthew 15:21–28.

6. John 5:14.

7. Jonathan Edwards, "The True Excellency of a Gospel Minister," in *The Works of Jonathan Edwards*, vol. 2 (Edinburgh: Banner of Truth Trust, 1974), 958.

8. 2 Corinthians 6:3.

9. 1 Corinthians 4:16; 1 Corinthians 11:1.

10. Philippians 3:17.

11. Philippians 4:9.

12. Hebrews 13:7.

13. Philip H. Towner, *1–2 Timothy and Titus* (Downers Grove, IL: InterVarsity, 1994), 82.

14. Joseph H. Thayer, *Thayer's Greek-English Lexicon of the New Testament* (Grand Rapids: Baker Book House, 1977), 632.

15. 2 Peter 2:13–14, 19.

16. 2 Peter 2:15.

17. Numbers 22–24.

18. John 12:49–53.

19. Spurgeon, *Lectures to My Students*, 9.

Chapter 3 In View of His Appearing

1. Ezekiel 3:17–19.

2. Acts 20:26–27.

3. Spurgeon, *Lectures to My Students*, 309.

4. 2 Timothy 4:16.

5. 2 Corinthians 5:10.

6. Spurgeon, *Lectures to My Students*, 12.

7. Gordon D. Fee, *The First Epistle to the Corinthians* (Grand Rapids: Eerdmans, 1987), 145.

8. 1 Corinthians 9:25–27.

9. 2 Timothy 4:7–8.

10. James 3:1.

11. 1 Peter 5:4.

Chapter 4 Above Reproach

1. *Epigraph*. Henry Ward Beecher, *Yale Lectures on Preaching* (New York: J. B. Ford and Company, 1872), 37.

2. 1 John 1:8, 10.

3. Proverbs 20:9.

4. 1 Timothy 4:12–15.

5. 1 Timothy 3:2.

6. Thayer, *Thayer's Greek-English Lexicon of the New Testament*, 44.

7. W. Robertson Nicoll, ed., *The Expositor's Greek Testament*, vol. 4 (Grand Rapids: Eerdmans, 1965), 111.

8. John Calvin, "Commentaries on the Epistles to Timothy, Titus, and Philemon," in *Calvin's Commentaries*, vol. 21 (1974 repr.; Grand Rapids: Baker Book House, 2003), 79.

9. Towner, *1–2 Timothy and Titus*, 229.

10. Matthew 7:16–17.

Chapter 5 Humility

1. *Epigraph*. Richard Baxter, *The Reformed Pastor*, ed. James M. Houston (Portland, OR: Multnomah, 1982), 18.

2. William Barclay, *The Letters to Timothy, Titus and Philemon* (Philadelphia: Westminster, 1960), 289–90.

3. Ibid., 289.

4. James Denney, *Studies in Theology* (Grand Rapids: Baker Book House, 1976), 161.

5. Spurgeon, *Lectures to My Students*, 48.

6. W. E. Sangster, *Power in Preaching* (Nashville: Abingdon, 1958), 106–7.

7. Quoted in Charles Bridges, *The Christian Ministry* (Carlisle, PA: Banner of Truth Trust, 1967), 152.

8. John R. W. Stott, *The Preacher's Portrait* (Grand Rapids: Eerdmans, 1961), 77.

9. 1 Corinthians 15:9; Ephesians 3:8; 1 Timothy 1:15.

10. Philippians 3:4–6.

11. Andrew A. Bonar, *Memoir and Remains of Robert Murray M'Cheyne* (Edinburgh: Banner of Truth, 1995), 281.

Chapter 6 Contentment

1. *Epigraph*. Charles Edward Jefferson, *Quiet Hints to Growing Preachers in My Study* (New York: Thomas Y. Crowell & Co., 1901), 134.

2. Deuteronomy 5:21.

3. Genesis 3:1–6.

4. Ephesians 5:5.

5. 1 Peter 5:2.

6. Acts 16:8–10.

7. 1 Thessalonians 2:9.

8. 1 Timothy 6:3–5.

9. Luke 12:15.

10. Matthew 6:19–20.

11. Luke 17:7–10.

Chapter 7 Fidelity to God's Word

1. *Epigraph*. Stott, *The Preacher's Portrait*, 15.

2. Romans 10:14, 17.

3. John 17:17.

4. 2 Corinthians 5:19–20.

5. NASB.

6. Stott, *The Preacher's Portrait*, 17.

7. 2 Timothy 1:13–14.

8. Acts 20:26–27.

9. 2 Corinthians 4:2.

10. 2 Timothy 2:15.

11. Bridges, *The Christian Ministry*, 107.

12. Quoted in Melville D. Landon, *Kings of the Platform and Pulpit* (Chicago: F. C. Smedley & Co., 1892), 417.

13. Baxter, *The Reformed Pastor*, 14.

14. Raymond W. McLaughlin, *The Ethics of Persuasive Preaching* (Grand Rapids: Baker Book House, 1979), 193.

Chapter 8 Courage

1. *Epigraph.* Bridges, *The Christian Ministry*, 126.

2. Isaiah 30:9–11.

3. Micah 2:11.

4. Bridges, *The Christian Ministry*, 123.

5. McLaughlin, *The Ethics of Persuasive Preaching*, 194.

6. Ibid., 150.

7. Exodus 4:10–14.

8. Jeremiah 1:8.

9. Acts 18:9; Acts 23:11.

10. Matthew 10:28.

11. Bridges, *The Christian Ministry*, 126.

12. 2 Timothy 1:8–12.

13. Galatians 1:10.

14. 1 Thessalonians 2:4.

15. Ephesians 4:15.

16. Bonar, *Memoir and Remains of Robert Murray M'Cheyne*, 403.

Chapter 9 Purity of Life

1. *Epigraph.* Stanley J. Grenz and Roy D. Bell, *Betrayal of Trust* (Downers Grove, IL: InterVarsity, 1995), 36.

2. Gene A. Getz, *The Measure of a Man* (Ventura, CA: Regal, 1995), 45.

3. 2 Timothy 2:22.

4. Author unnamed, "How Common Is Pastoral Indiscretion?" *Leadership* 9, no. 1 (Winter 1988): 12.

5. 1 Timothy 3:2, 7.

6. Grenz and Bell, *Betrayal of Trust*, 34.

7. Spurgeon, *Lectures to My Students*, 13–14.

8. 1 Corinthians 10:12.

Chapter 10 Purity of Mind

1. Grenz and Bell, *Betrayal of Trust*, 59.

2. Author unnamed, "Pastors Viewing Internet Pornography: How Widespread Is It?" *Leadership* 22, no. 1 (Winter 2001): 89.

3. Ibid., 94.

4. There is help for you. A list of resources for those struggling with pornography can be found on page 93 of the Winter 2002 issue of *Leadership*. Another list is available on page 45 of the March 5, 2001, issue of *Christianity Today*.

5. Luke 6:39–40.

6. Quoted in Christine J. Gardner, "Tangled in the Worst of the Web," *Christianity Today* 45, no. 4 (March 5, 2001), 49.

Chapter 11 Temperance

1. *Epigraph.* Jonathan Edwards, "Memoirs of Jonathan Edwards," in *The Works of Jonathan Edwards*, vol. 1 (Edinburgh: Banner of Truth Trust, 1974), xx.

2. Ray Furr, "Christian Pastor More Likely to Be Overweight," *Biblical Recorder* September 6, 2002, http://www.biblical recorder.org/content/news/2002/9_6_2002/ne060902christian.shtml (accessed January 17, 2003).

3. Toby Druin, "Kenneth Cooper: Dr. Aerobics," *The Baptist Standard*, April 8, 2002, http://www.baptiststandard.com/2002/4_8/print/cooper_kenneth.html (accessed January 17, 2003).

4. If Paul was using the word "temperate" as a reference only to moderation in the use of alcohol, he would be repeating himself in the next verse, where he goes on to say that an elder must be one who is "not given to drunkenness."

5. Warren W. Wiersbe, *The Bible Exposition Commentary*, vol. 2 (Wheaton: Victor Books, 1989), 737.

6. Robert C. Anderson, *The Effective Pastor* (Chicago: Moody, 1985), 7.

7. Furr, "Christian Pastor More Likely to Be Overweight."

8. Kenneth Cooper, *Faith-Based Fitness* (Nashville: Thomas Nelson, 1995), 14.

9. 1 Timothy 4:3–5.

10. United States Department of Health and Human Services, "Overweight and Obesity Threaten U.S. Health Gains," news release, December 13, 2001, http://www.surgeon general.gov/news/pressreleases/pr_obesity.htm (accessed January 24, 2003).

11. 1 Corinthians 10:31.

12. Arthur S. Hoyt, *The Preacher: His Person, Message, and Method* (Cincinnati: Jennings and Graham, 1909), 47.

13. American Obesity Association, "Obesity in the U.S.," AOA Fact Sheet, http://www .obesity.org/subs/fastfacts/obesity_US.shtml (accessed January 24, 2003).

14. United States Department of Health and Human Services, "Overweight and Obesity Threaten U.S. Health Gains."

15. John N. Burry, "Obesity and Virtue. Is Staying Lean a Matter of Ethics?" *Medical Journal of Australia* 171 (1999): 609–10.

16. One of the most helpful websites in choosing a weight-loss plan is that sponsored by the American Obesity Association at www .obesity.org. This site provides general information on overweight and obesity, weight-loss strategies, and evaluations of many legitimate diets and weight-loss organizations.

17. Toby Druin, "Kenneth Cooper: Dr. Aerobics."

Chapter 12 Practicing Spiritual Disciplines

1. *Epigraph.* Dallas Willard, *The Spirit of the Disciplines* (San Francisco: Harper, 1988), 126.

2. Richard J. Foster, *Celebration of Discipline* (San Francisco: Harper, 1988), 7–8.

3. Jonathan Edwards, *The Works of Jonathan Edwards*, vol. 1 (Edinburgh: Banner of Truth Trust, 1974), xx.

4. Romans 1:9–10.

5. Ephesians 1:16.

6. C. Peter Wagner, *Prayer Shield* (Ventura, CA: Regal, 1992), 78–79.

7. Foster, *Celebration of Discipline*, 35.

8. Spurgeon, *Lectures to My Students*, 42.

9. Matthew 5:16–18.

10. Foster, *Celebration of Discipline*, 16.

11. Eugene H. Peterson, *Working the Angles* (Grand Rapids: Eerdmans, 1998), 16–17.

Chapter 13 The Practice of Expository Preaching

1. *Epigraph.* H. B. London Jr. and Neil B. Wiseman, *The Heart of a Great Pastor* (Ventura, CA: Regal, 1994), 177.

2. Bonar, *Memoir and Remains of Robert Murray M'Cheyne*, 281.

3. Haddon W. Robinson, *Biblical Preaching*, 2nd ed. (Grand Rapids: Baker Academic, 2002), 21.

4. Ibid., 22.

5. Stott, *The Preacher's Portrait*, 31.

6. Robinson, *Biblical Preaching*, 26.

7. Bridges, *The Christian Ministry*, 162.

8. Ibid., 157–58.

Chapter 14 Growing by Staying

1. *Epigraph.* Jefferson, *Quiet Hints to Growing Preachers*, 139.

2. Jeanette Gardner Littleton, "The Displaced Parsonage," *Your Church* (November/December 1999): 70.

3. John Calvin, *Institutes of the Christian Religion*, vol. 2, ed. John T. McNeill, trans. Ford Lewis Battles, The Library of Christian Classics (Philadelphia: Westminster, 1967), 1060.

4. Bonar, *Memoir and Remains of Robert Murray M'Cheyne*, 68.

5. David F. Wells, *No Place for Truth* (Grand Rapids: Eerdmans, 1994), 229.

6. Ibid., 228.

7. Jefferson, *Quiet Hints to Growing Preachers*, 139–40.

8. Ibid., 140.

9. Wells, *No Place for Truth*, 231.

10. Eugene H. Peterson, *Under the Unpredictable Plant* (Grand Rapids: Eerdmans, 1994), 20.

11. Haddon Robinson, "What Authority Do We Have Anymore?" *Leadership* 13, no. 2 (Spring 1992): 29.

12. Eric Reed, "The Preaching Report Card," *Leadership* 20, no. 3 (Summer 1999): 87.

13. Peterson, *Under the Unpredictable Plant*, 21.

14. Jefferson, *Quiet Hints to Growing Preachers*, 140–41.

Conclusion

1. Bridges, *The Christian Ministry*, 159.

Appendix Voices from the Past

1. Clement, "The First Epistle of the Blessed Clement, The Disciple of Peter the Apostle," chap. 8, in *Ante-Nicene Fathers*, ed. Alexander Roberts and James Donaldson, trans. B. P. Pratten (Grand Rapids: Eerdmans, 1951), 8:60.

2. Peter, Archbishop of Alexandria, "The Canons of the Blessed Peter, Archbishop of Alexandria, as They Are Given in His Sermons on Penitence," canon 10, in *Ante-Nicene Fathers*, ed. Alexander Roberts and James Donaldson, trans. James B. H. Hawkins (Grand Rapids: Eerdmans, 1957), 6:274.

3. St. Chrysostom, "Homily 13, 1 Timothy 4:11–14," in *Nicene and Post Nicene Fathers of the Christian Church*, ed. and trans. Philip Schaff (Grand Rapids: Eerdmans, 1956), 13:449.

4. St. Chrysostom, "Homily 4, Titus 2:2–5" in *Nicene and Post-Nicene Fathers of the Christian Church*, 1st series, ed. and trans. Philip Schaff (Grand Rapids: Eerdmans, 1956), 13:533.

5. St. Chrysostom, "Homily 72, Matt. 23:1–3," in *Nicene and Post-Nicene Fathers*, 1st series, ed. Philip Schaff, trans. Sir George Prevost, Baronet (Grand Rapids: Eerdmans, 1956), 10:436.

6. Ibid., 436.

7. Martin Luther, "Lectures on Titus" in *Luther's Works*, ed. Jaroslav Pelikan and Walter A. Hansen (St. Louis: Concordia Publishing House, 1955), 29:59.

8. Calvin, *Institutes of the Christian Religion*, vol. 2, 1063.

9. John Calvin, "Commentaries on the Epistles to Timothy, Titus, and Philemon" (Grand Rapids: Eerdmans, 1948), 313.

10. William Ames, *The Marrow of Theology* (Durham, NC: The Labyrinth Press, 1968), 191.

11. Baxter, *The Reformed Pastor*, 32.

12. Ibid., 33.

13. Philip Jacob Spener, *Pia Desideria*, trans. and ed. Theodore G. Tappert (Philadelphia: Fortress Press, 1964), 107–8.

14. Jonathan Edwards, "The True Excellency of a Gospel Minister," in *The Works of Jonathan Edwards*, vol. 2, 958.

15. John Wesley, *Works of John Wesley*, vol. 7 (New York: 1831), 229, quoted in James L. Golden, Berquist F. Goodwin, and William E. Coleman, *The Rhetoric of Western Thought* (Dubuque, IA: Kendall/Hunt Publishing Company, 1983), 297.

16. A. Vinet, *Pastoral Theology*, trans. and ed. Thomas H. Skinner (New York: Harper and Brothers, 1853), 193.

17. Bridges, *The Christian Ministry*, 158.

18. Ibid., 159.

19. Ibid., 157.

20. Bonar, *Memoir and Remains of Robert Murray M'Cheyne*, 406–7.

21. Ibid., 282.

22. Beecher, *Yale Lectures on Preaching*, 37.

23. Ibid., 39.

24. Brooks, *Lectures on Preaching*, 49.

25. Ibid., 51.

26. Spurgeon, *Lectures to My Students*, 11.

27. Ibid., 9.

28. E. M. Bounds, *Power through Prayer* (Springdale, PA: Whitaker House, 1982), 8.

29. Ibid., 67.

30. Ibid., 69.

31. Ibid., 31.

32. Ibid., 36.

33. Ibid., 9–10.

Dean Shriver (D.Min., Gordon-Conwell Theological Seminary) is founding pastor of Intermountain Baptist Church. *Nobody's Perfect, but You Have to Be* is Shriver's first book, growing from his eighteen years in pastoral ministry. He lives in Salt Lake City, Utah.